FOLLOWING GOD'S PLAN FOR YOUR LIFE SERIES

BECOMING A PERSON OF PURPOSE

E.E. EGILA

FOREWORD BY DR. JOHN AKPAMI

WHAT PEOPLE ARE SAYING ABOUT THE BOOK

Pastor EE Egila intelligently, comprehensively and profoundly captured the original purpose for the essence of humanity and demystified the drama around finding, following and fulfilling God's plan for one's life, particularly in a world of meaninglessness and confusion.

He further communicates clearly the tremendous power of unlocking one's identity in Christ, as one of the keys to enjoying a victorious and successful life. This is not just another book; it is a masterpiece and a compendium of kingdom truths, responsible for maximizing one's God-given potential while actualizing God's purpose for one in life, business and ministry.

I highly recommend this book to every young man and woman, emerging leaders in the church and marketplace; and established leaders who desire to train others to find, follow and fulfill God's plan and purpose for their lives.

-Steven Edward
CEO, School of Self-discovery & Leadershift, Author and Conference Speaker.

Reading through this book, I am unable to comment on it better than it was captured in the words of the author. These words sum up this book in the best way, hear him:

'I wrote this book out of a burning passion in my heart to see you become all you were created to be. I desire to see you follow God's divine plan for your life. What you have in your hands is not just another motivational, psychological book on how to fulfil your destiny. It is not a book on how to become a millionaire or win your world. This book is about something far greater, something so important in the heart of God. In fact, it is the heartbeat of God. God wants you to follow His plan for your life.'

I commend this book for the style employed; it breaks down the body of knowledge required to fulfil destiny in such an easy-to-read manner that you will find it easy to digest. I highly recommend this book to the young, it will help them make less mistakes and fulfil their destiny with precision. I recommend it to the old, it will help you review your life and ensure it aligns with God's will for you.

-Ocholi Okutepa
Co-Pioneer, Relationship and Marriage Outreach, Author and Conference Speaker.

The subject of purpose and its discovery seems to have been an over flogged topic in the body of Christ, especially since its rise to prominence in recent charismatic ministries. On the shoulders of great servants of God, it has become a significant emphasis. However, I have found something unique about this book, particularly an aspect that must be a major addition to the study of the subject.

What has intrigued me about this reading is the great simplicity, academic layout, and thorough coverage of the subject of purpose with deep insight into the pathway of discovery.

Pastor Egila has uniquely covered a major frontier in the subject of purpose, by addressing areas of traditional beliefs and experiences that have been a stronghold, keeping many from attempting to uncover God's intentional plan for their lives. This is because they have embraced false definitions, that are not in alignment with God's plan as their identity before discussing the subject. Scripture warns against forcing new wine into old wineskins (Mark 2:22), and what I see here is the thorough addressing of the wineskin before the release of new wine, which I believe to be the mastery of the divine pathway to arriving at God's plan for your life.

Enjoy an amazing read, and when you are done, you will agree with me that you are blessed, if you pay attention to this beautiful work and reading experience.

Shalom.

Yours in Christ,

-Pastor Chingtok Ishaku.

Senior Pastor of The Godlife Assembly, Nigeria

I have known Pastor E.E. Egila for about three (3) decades now, since growing up together as friends in a suburb in Makurdi, Benue State, and one thing has been consistent with him is the issue of purpose.

He has focused on the matter of purpose passionately from our early days, until we nicknamed him the "Apostle of Purpose." Going through the pages of this book, I wasn't slightly surprised because the author's consistency about purpose, has produced a rich purpose manual today.

In this edition, he has succinctly, yet in good detail, X-rayed the subject of purpose from discovery to deployment. Suffice it to say, among many other books on purpose, this stands out for its simplicity and clarity.

I recommend this manual to every young person, who is interested in living a purposeful life and in getting the best result out of life.

Shalom!

Oche Jonkings
Music Minister, Preacher, Businessman, President, Royal Rhythm Music

E.E. EGILA

FOREWORD BY DR JOHN AKPAMI

BECOMING A PERSON OF PURPOSE

ISBN: 978-978-60396-4-0

Connect with E.E EG⍰LA
Phone: +2348035679980, +447747054807
Email: emmanuel.egila1@gmail.com
(Facebook) @Emmanuel Esuga Egila
(Telegram) @eeegila www.facebook.com /egila
(Website) https://www.emmanuelegila.org

Cover design by Zoodex Media +2348132077963
Layout design by Joel Ibrahim +2347037108385
Typesetting by Elmond Isaiah +2348067370005

Printed and published in Nigeria by
Impact Empire Limited +2347037108385

TABLE OF CONTENTS

DEDICATION

This book is dedicated to the man and woman who passionately desire to become a person of purpose and fulfill God's plan for their lives.

ACKNOWLEDGEMENTS

My greatest appreciation is to my Lord and Saviour, Jesus Christ, who has shown me so much mercy, grace and help in becoming a person of purpose.

I am grateful to my wife, sweetheart, and priority, Ene for her understanding and support over the years. Thank you for being a great help to me. It's been a sweet journey fulfilling purpose with you. Thank you to my son, Ellis, for being an amazing son and growing into a person of purpose daily.

I appreciate the priceless role of Dr. John Esuga Akpami in my life and in writing this book. Thank you for the invaluable practical tips for life and ministry you always give me. I am forever grateful.

I specially appreciate my pastor and mentor, Reverend Joshua Tende, who by precept and example, has demonstrated his trust in me time and time again, and mentored me into fulfilling God's purpose for my life.

I appreciate Apostle OSA Aiyemo, for his guidance and relevant counsels that have become timeless pillars of support and accurate compass for navigating life's vast vicissitudes.

Honour and acknowledgements to all who shaped this book – even those who had no idea they were being used of God to help. Special thanks to Pastor Chingtok Ishaku, Pastor Ocholi Okutepa, Pastor Steve Edwards and Oche Johnkings who read, gave feedback, prayed and encouraged me all the way.

Special thank you to Joel Ibrahim, Shaala Abraham, Joy Yor, Michael Eugene, Elmond Isaiah, Pastor Afolabi Ibrahim and Rev. Felix Afolabi for all the great sacrifices and efforts towards producing this book. Thank you to Pastor Anointed Tende, Pastor Segun Alemede, Mr. and Mrs. Ibrahim and Christy Ambi, Mr. Endurance Igbinosun Agho for always believing in me.

FOREWORD

Lord, what will you have me to do? This was the question that Saul (who later became Paul) asked the Lord Jesus at his conversion on the way to Damascus.

Anyone who has come to know the Lord should also ask that question; "Lord, what is my life's purpose?" The answer to that question is what will give meaning to life. It becomes the pivot around which your future revolves. Life loses its quality without the discovery and pursuit of purpose. So engrossed was Paul in the pursuit of his life's purpose, that he could say in Acts 20:24; "But none of these things move me, neither count I my life dear unto myself, so that I might finish my course with joy and the ministry which I have received of the Lord Jesus to testify the gospel of the grace of God.

Paul, when he made this statement, had found something to live for, and if necessary, to die for.

The book, "Becoming a Person of Purpose" will not only help you to discover your life's purpose (the reason for your being) it will also help you live a life of impact.

Pastor Egila has laid out vital steps that will help the reader live a fulfilled life. It will prevent you from wearing shoes that are not your size or from running another man's race. It will help you overcome identity crisis and help you leave an indelible mark on the sands of time. Life will celebrate you as a precious gift to our world and the Body of Christ.

Shalom!

John Esuga Akpami, MBBS, PhD Senior Pastor
Christian Teaching Centre Family Church Zaria, Nigeria.

FOREWORD

The most important thing about your life in the sight of God is your God-given purpose, calling, and destiny.

Purpose gives meaning to your living and relevance to your existence. It simplifies your life, multiplies your effectiveness, and enhances your impact on other lives.

Therefore, the pursuit of purpose is the bedrock of successful living. So, you can measure your success in life by the pursuit of your purpose.

This truth explains why the book, "Becoming a Person of Purpose", by Pastor Egila is very priceless and timely. It will awaken the giant in you and sharpen your cutting edge in life.

I was privileged to read the manuscript of this book, and it blessed me richly. I strongly recommend this book to everyone who desires to live a profitable, fulfilling, and impactful life.

Read and study this book repeatedly, and you will be eternally grateful to God that you followed my advice.

Yours in service of the LORD,

Joshua K. A. Tende (PhD) The Senior Pastor,
The Father's Delight Int'l Ministry.

PREFACE

Your success in life is determined by your ability to know God's plan for your life and to fulfil it. Becoming a person of purpose is becoming that man that consistently follows God's plan for his life. The number one cause of failure in life, is failure to discover purpose. Many times, the reason people fail in life is because they do not follow God's original plan for their lives.

Destiny answers to purpose. It is not enough to live; one must live for something. The only reason you should desire to live should be because you have something to fulfil in this earth. When you don't know your life's mission, your life will be full of omissions. Why was I created? What did I come to do in this world? These are vital questions you must find answers to. Billy Graham once asked himself, "Who am I? What is my mission? Where am I going to? What am I here for?" Unless you can answer these questions like Billy Graham did, you may not be able to live as God wants you to. You will live a life of trials and errors, a life of so many omissions. It is a disaster not to know who you are and who you were created to be.

You need to pray seriously from your heart that you will not check out of this world without knowing and following God's plan for your life. Except you become a person of purpose by following God's plan for your life, you will end up being another man and doing another's man assignment. You were not created to fulfil your own ambition; you were created to do the will of God.

There are two kinds of people on earth today: those who are pursuing God's purpose for their lives by becoming people of purpose; and those who do what they want while pursuing their own agenda. You cannot become a person of purpose if you try to follow God with your senses, by mental assent or reading books. Purpose comes by revelation. If men knew what a beautiful destiny God has for them, they will abandon their own plans and follow God's plan for their lives.

> *For I know the plans I have for you; declares the Lord, plans to prosper you and not to harm you, plans to give you hope and a future. Then you will call upon me and come and pray to me, and I will listen to you. You will seek me and find me when you seek with all your heart. Jeremiah 29:11-13*

You must know that God always has your best interest at heart. He is not a liar. Believe Him when He says His plan is for good. In following God's plan for our lives, we justify the purpose for which we were born. Your life is not an experiment; it is an assignment. For most average individuals, becoming a person of purpose is just pursuing money, feeding the family, getting old and waiting to die! You have a far greater purpose in God's divine agenda.

I wrote this book out of a burning passion in my heart to see you become all you were created to be. I desire to see you follow God's divine plan for your life. What you have in your hands is not just another motivational, psychological book on how to fulfil your destiny. It is not a book on how to become a millionaire or win your world. This book is about something far greater, something so important in the heart of God. In fact, it is the heartbeat of God. God wants you to follow His plan for your life.

This book is a straight talk geared towards the release of God's purpose for your life. There must be a release of your purpose and the fulfillment of your destiny after the encounters with the revelations in this book. It is my prayer that before you check out of this world, you will accomplish the purpose of God for which you were born and that you will continue in the path of God's purpose for your life.

BECOMING A PERSON OF PURPOSE

CHAPTER ONE

LIVE FOR A PURPOSE

You were made with a manual – live up to it.

Genesis 1:26a

And God said, let us make man in our image, after our likeness…

The Almighty God is a purposeful God who, in His purposefulness, decided to create man in His own image. He made man in His original form. Man was created in the original nature of God. God is a God of *original*. Your birth into this world, no matter the circumstance and location, is a product of God's original intention. It was never an accidental occurrence, neither was it a product of chance, because God designed you to achieve something original. There is an original blueprint of God for your life. Billions of people are occupying this planet right now, living as photocopies and not in the original plan of God for their lives.

The commanding heights of God are only reached by men who understand the original intention of God for their lives. That you don't know God's purpose for your life does not mean God does not have a purpose for your life. There is an original blueprint of God for your life; it is only when you live according to this blueprint that you give God joy and pleasure for creating you. More so, it is only by following that original blueprint that we can find true success in life and destiny. You were not created to do what you want with your life. You were created to be who God wants you to be. Some people are busy fulfilling the purposes of men for their lives while abandoning God's original plan for them.

You were created unique and in God's original design. You are ONE IN A BILLION. You are unique and God created you special. Psalm 139:15 – 18 (TLB) Says:

> *You were there while I was being formed in utter seclusion. You saw me before I was born and scheduled each day of my life before I began to breathe. Every day was recorded in your book!*

My beloved wife, Dr. Ene Egila, once explained the process of conception to me. She said that during the process of conception, millions (20–100 million) male seeds struggle to fertilize the female egg, and only one completes the process. You are that one victorious cell!

God said He knew you right from when He was forming you, and already recorded your purpose in His book. Philosophers and psychologists have tried to tackle the looming question of purpose with largely unsatisfactory answers. Countless dollars are spent on our search for purpose in life, but thanks be to God, we have access to our purpose through the guidance of the Holy Spirit.

God works on purpose. It is an insult to the intelligence and excellence of God to think that He created you without any reason and plan for your life. You were not created to make the numbers. You are a product of His predetermined counsel and purpose. See what Jeremiah 1:5 (NLT) says:

> *I knew you before I formed you in your mother's womb. Before you were born, I set you apart and appointed you as my prophet to the nations.*

God has an agenda He wants you to carry out, He created you to bring it to fruition. Your life is not an experiment; it is an assignment. God is the reason behind your creation. He started your creation from His mind. You were necessary, that is why God created you. Ecclesiastes 3:11, 14 says:

> *He hath made everything beautiful in His time; also, he hath set the world in their heart, so that no man can find out the work that God maketh from the beginning to the end.*
>
> *I know that whatsoever God doeth, it shall be forever; nothing can be put to it, nor anything taken from it: and God doeth it, that men should fear before Him.*

There is nobody like you in this world. No two human beings are the same. Even the most identical twins are still not the same. God had a plan for your life before He created you. God is not a purposeless God. He does everything with a purpose and agenda. You're not here on this planet because a man and a woman slept together. That was only part of God's ground plan for your life. A man and woman had to sleep together, because you had to be here. You're here for God's divine purpose. Your life is not about you, but about giving glory and pleasure to our Father God.

Many people in this world are living purposeless lives even though they were created by a purposeful God. They really can't tell where they are going in life. So many famous persons have reached the top of their fields only to realize they were never in the original plan of God for their lives. That shall not be your case after reading this book. A life with no purpose is not the reason why God created you. As God's child, it is your right to know His purpose for your life. As a child of God when people ask you "Where are you going?" your response should be resolute, unwavering and full of assurance that you know where God is leading you to.

I love this response by Jesus in John 8:14

> *Even if I testify on my own behalf, my testimony is valid, for I know where I came from and where I am going. But you have no idea where I come from or where I am going.*

Jesus made this bold assertion because He operated with full understanding of the clear assignment God gave Him. Don't live this life trying to survive. Survival is never the reason for life. Pastor Rick Warren once said that most people live out their lives in one of the following three levels:

1. **Survival:** Here, they simply just exist with no sense of meaning and purpose for their lives. They lack zeal and passion to live a meaningful life. No purpose, no goals, no hope; just existence. I like to call it existence without meaning. They simply live to eat and wait to die. They continue living simply because their hearts are still beating, and they are still breathing. What a waste of life and existence! They live life just to make up the number for census purposes.

2. **Success:** At this level people live for just material possession; collecting and possessing more and more. They work for a living: paycheck to paycheck. People at this level are never satisfied with their material possessions. They want new cars, new houses, new clothes, etc., and that is all that life consists of for them. In a materialistic society, people in this group are highly celebrated and admired. People at this level don't mind working two or three jobs, not because they must, but for the finer things of life. Most Christians at this level put the things of life ahead of their love for God. They have difficulty finding time for the study of God's Word and prayers. Greed and covetousness rule them. Luke 12:15 says, "Take heed, beware of covetousness, for one's life does not consist in the abundance of the things he possesses".

   It is amazing that Jesus used the phrase "take heed". This is because a lot of people have been consumed by greed and covetousness. This is not to say we should have poverty mentality, but we should desire to move to a greater level with God, in the pursuit of His divine assignment for our lives. In the rat race of life, the problem is that even if you win, you are still a rat.

3. **Significance:** This is the level God wants us to be. At this level, we view life from the perspective of God. At this level, we are obsessed with pleasing God and doing all that He created us for. This is not just mere existence and survival or even success, it is about significance. Significance makes you know that your life matters; that it counts for something and is pleasing to God. Living with significance in focus honors and glorifies God.

Every time you seek significance in life and destiny, you are seeking to give full expression to the purpose of God for your life and destiny. When all you desire is to make a difference in the lives of others and bring glory to God, you are becoming a person of purpose. 1Cor. 10:31 says:

Therefore, whether you eat or drink, or whatever you do, do all to the glory of God.

When all you seek and desire in life is to glorify God, you are a person of purpose. When you discover significance, you have discovered God's purpose for your life. If glorifying God becomes your vision and obsession, then you are a man or woman of significant impact in your generation. Becoming a person of purpose is seeking to give full expression to the reason why God originally created you as this is what gives Him glory. Hebrew 13:21(NKJV) says:

make you complete in every good work to do His will,

working in you that which is well pleasing in His sight, through Jesus Christ, to whom be glory forever and ever. **Amen.**

You don't seek to fulfil your divine destiny for material possession or to become famous, but to please our Father, God. You are not seeking the glory of God when you are living life just for yourself. Always ask yourself of what significance what you are about to do will be to man and God. Always ask yourself will this thought, word or deed better the lives of others and glorify God? 1 Peter 4:11 says, "If any man speaks, let him speak as the oracles of God; if any man minister, let him do it as of the ability which God giveth: that God in all things may be glorified through Jesus Christ, to whom be praise and dominion for ever and ever. Amen.

Every man wants to be relevant and significant in our world. People want to find satisfaction in themselves and be the best they were created to be, yet only few have come to the realization that God created them to be different from others. God has designed you to achieve a specific purpose on earth. Have you ever asked yourself what your assignment is on earth? Have you ever considered what you were sent to this world to accomplish? What is the intent and the purpose of God for creating you? What is your life mission? Whom are you sent to? What is in the mind of the creator for sending you here? The answer to the above questions is PURPOSE.

WHAT IS PURPOSE?

Purpose is the result or the objective that necessitated the creation or design of something. It is also the reason for doing something. Every product on earth was preceded by a purpose. Every creator defines the purpose of his product.

What is your purpose?

Your purpose is the reason God sent you to this world. Your purpose is what was in God's mind before He created you. Jeremiah 1:5 [NLT] captures it better:

> *I knew you before I formed you in your mother's womb, before you were born, I set you apart and appointed you as my prophet to the nations*

God created you to answer a question. Everybody is on earth to answer a question. The greatest tragedy in life is to go through life not knowing what was in the mind of God before He created you. You will not amount to true greatness in life without giving full expression to why God created you. When you don't know God's purpose for your life, your life becomes meaningless, worthless, dishonourable and full of victimization. See what God told Kenneth. E Hagin in a vision in 1987:

> *"Even when men get my plan, Jesus said to me in that early morning visitation of 1987, oftentimes their purposes are wrong. 'Some people get my plan', JESUS said, 'I speak to them, but in trying to carry out that plan, their purpose become wrong. So, I cannot bless them because man's purpose and pursuits must line up with my plan and purpose for the fullness of my blessing."*

If we learn to follow God's purpose for our lives, then we will have true success in life and destiny. I like what Dale Carpenter said: "Real success in life is knowing what GOD wants you to do and doing it". Everything about your life is tied to God's purpose for your life. No wonder Dr Paul Enenche once said, "The purpose of life is a life of purpose." Becoming a person of purpose has to do with knowing the reason why God created you and walking toward the fulfillment of that reason. It is a disaster not to know what God's plan for your life is. Becoming a person of purpose means being aware of the reason why you are alive. No one has eternity to fulfil destiny. It becomes very important for one to live this life with a purpose mentality.

It is knowing God's purpose for our lives that gives our lives meaning and value. When you understand the "why" of existence, you go about life daily with that understanding. You cannot run this life on your own terms and conditions. God has a program for your life. Understanding why God created you is one of the most important things you must do in life. It helps you become the best you were created to be and sets you in motion to live a fulfilled life.

Contrary to popular belief, Dr. Myles Munroe says, "The wealthiest places on earth are not the oil fields in the Middle East or the gold or diamond mines of South Africa. The wealthiest places on planet earth are the cemeteries". Buried in cemeteries are authors that never became one, pastors that never preached a sermon, and singers that never wrote and sang a song. Buried in the cemeteries are books that will never be written, dreams that will never be fulfilled and ideas that will never be spoken. Cemeteries are places of buried visions and songs that will never find expression. People take to the graves their dreams and passions. Great businesses are forever lost, there are houses that will never be built. Ministries and churches have been swallowed up on the earth. People die with the awesome purposes of God for their lives.

God has deposited something great in you, and His purpose for creating you is that you die giving all His rich deposits in you to the world. Seek to impact your world by following God's plan for your life. Becoming a person of purpose is finding out the "why" of your existence and fulfilling it. Until you know the "why" of your existence, you cannot be a person of purpose.

When the mother eagle lays her eggs, she does so in a nest high up in the sky. When the eggs hatch, she begins to feed the little eaglets until they grow and develop wings. Albeit the little eaglets cannot fly on their own even with their wings fully developed because they do not know the purpose of their wings. One day, the mother eagle drags each eaglet out of the nest and forces it to fly. It is then that the eaglet begins to fly on its own having now discovered the purpose of its wings. It is now that you are alive and reading this book that you can discover or live for a purpose. No wonder Horace Mann said, "Be ashamed to die until you've won some victory for humanity."

> *And he trembling and astonished said, Lord, what will you have me do? And the Lord said unto him; Arise and go into the city, and it shall be told you what you must do* (Acts 9:6)

Apostle Paul asked a very important question when the Lord Jesus appeared to him on his way to Damascus. "Lord what will you have me to do?" It is a question we must ask daily if we are to become a people of purpose. The good thing is, every time you ask God "What will you have me to do?" God will always give you direction. He answered Paul in Acts 26:16 – 18:

> *But I have appeared unto thee for this purpose; to make thee minister and a witness both of these things which thou hast seen, and of those things in the world I will appear unto thee. Delivering thee from the people and from the gentiles unto which now I send thee to open their eyes, and turn them from darkness to light, and from the power of Satan unto God, that they may receive forgiveness of sins and inheritance among them which are sanctified by faith that is in me.*

Paul lived his life completely in obedience to this divine agenda. He completely pursued God's purpose for his life and lived the rest of his life pleasing God. I believe one of the reason Paul succeeded more than many of his contemporaries was because he immediately followed God's purpose for his life after his conversion. No wonder he said, "I have fought a good fight, I have finished my course, I have kept the faith."

The most important thing in life is to serve the purpose for which you were fashioned by God. To be outstanding in your generation is to know why God created you. Until you live for a purpose, your life will be meaningless to many.

You don't achieve anything great in life by chance or by accident. Great accomplishments in life are a product of purpose. Purpose shows you your special uniqueness and shows you that there is something you have to offer your generation that no one else can offer. Becoming a person of purpose creates in you a desire to be original. If you realize that there is something in you that is not in any other person, your life will become more meaningful. When you don't understand God's purpose for your life you will struggle to be original. Many people are unable to identify where they uniquely belong in life because they fail to see the original blueprint of God for their lives. When you live a life of purpose, you don't envy anybody because you know there is enough space in the air for men of purpose to fly. Bishop David Oyedepo once asked, "Have you ever seen two birds colliding in the air for lack of space?" It's impossible!

CHAPTER TWO

WHO ARE YOU?
A DISCOVERY

Knowing who you are is the key to becoming what God wants you to become. Knowing who you are is the route to becoming a person of purpose. Do you know who you are? Are people around you aware of who you are? Do your friends know the reason you were born? If we called upon your friends right now, could they tell us your life purpose in a word or two? Mathew 16:13 says "when Jesus came to the region of Caesarea Philippi, He asked his disciples, "Who do people say the son of man is?" A person of purpose is that person who truly knows who he is, and whom others around him can give the same testimony. Ignorance of your identity is a major reason for failure in life. John the Baptist understood what his life assignment was. He knew he was a voice not an echo of another man.

> *Then they said to him, "Who are you, that we may give an answer to those who sent us what do you say about yourself?".*
>
> *He said: "I am the voice of one crying in the*

wilderness: make straight the way of the Lord. John 1:22 – 23 (NKJV)

You must get to a point where you can answer with clarity and boldness what you are created to do. Most times, when you ask people, "Who are you?" they give a completely different answer from what God created them to be. The simple reason is they are seeing themselves different from how God sees them. Unless you can answer this question clearly, you may not be able to live as God wants you to. You will live a life of trial and error, a life of so many omissions. Men are frustrated today because they don't know who they are, ignorance of your identity in God is a major reason for a life of struggle. When a man is busy doing what he is not created to do, I could hear God asking him, "Is that who you are? Is that what I created you to be? Is this your place?"

A major problem in the world today is the identity crisis. Many people don't know who they are. They are still grappling with the question, "Who am I? What am I doing on earth? What's my life about?" There are great discoveries that men have made, but the greatest discoveries that anyone could ever make is SELF DISCOVERY. There is no greater discovery than that.

TO KNOW WHO YOU ARE, IT IS IMPORTANT TO KNOW WHO YOU ARE NOT.

1. WHO YOU ARE IS NOT THE NAME YOU WERE GIVEN AT BIRTH

Your name is good, but who you are is more than the name you were given at birth. It is good to bear a name, but who you are is not defined completely by the name you were given at birth. Some people eventually do a name change but that does not mean that they have changed who God created them to be. Many people mention their name when they are asked "Who are you?" You are more than your name. In Genesis 32:22-30, we see Jacob trying to define who he was by the name he was given.

The devil will try to confuse you to ignore your identity by limiting it to just your name. Most times people are named based on the circumstances surrounding their birth. You are far more than the circumstances surrounding your birth. One of Satan's strategies is to get you to be completely ignorant of your identity. YOU EXISTED BEFORE YOU GOT THE NAME. If the devil can succeed in making you doubt your identity, he has succeeded indeed.

> *Now when the tempter came to Him," he said "if you are the Son of God, command that these stones become bread.* Mathew 4:3

This was the devil's attempt to make Jesus doubt His identity. The devil thought that he could confuse Jesus by saying, "If thou be the Son of God". Truly, Jesus was the son of God. He came to fulfil God's purpose, and the devil wanted to confuse Him the same way he confused the first man in the Garden of Eden.

Names can affect destiny, but you are not the name given to you at birth. Some people even call themselves what does not agree with what God created them to be. They take on names like "I am a sinner", "I am unworthy", "I am bad", "I am unfit", "I am sick", etc. You are not the negative names you call yourself. Don't let your name define your destiny. You cannot call a dog a human simply because it is wearing a dress.

When John the Baptist was asked, "Who are you?" he did not answer them by saying, "I am John", but he told them "I am the voice of one crying." John was a voice and not just a name.

> *No longer shall your name be called Abram, but your name shall be Abraham; for I have made you a father of many nations.*
>
> *Then God said to Abraham, as for Sarai your wife, you shall call her name Sarai, but Sarah shall be her name.* (Genesis 17:5, 15)

God made Abraham, father of many nations even before he was named Abraham. My point is, look beyond your name to discover who God made you. Sometimes your name may be a title you received or one that was given by men, but you are more than just a name.

2. WHO YOU ARE IS NOT WHERE YOU ARE FROM (ORIGIN, FAMILY, RACE, OR NATIONALITY)

Your family, origin, race, tribe, ethnicity or nation does not determine who you are. You discover and find your identity outside of all this. Some people consider themselves disadvantaged in life because of where and how they were born. Your family background does not reflect who you are and what God created you to be. You don't have the same destiny as the destiny of your family members, tribe or race. You don't have to end up like your biological father or mother. You don't have to become like anyone. The right to discover who you are lies with you.

In Genesis 32:24, a man wrestled with Jacob to disconnect him from seeing himself based on where he was coming from, his race, his tribe and origin. You fulfil destiny alone and not with people of your family, nation or tribe.

> *Then the lord turned to him and said, go in this might of yours and you shall save Israel from the hands of the Midianites.*
>
> *Have I not sent you? So, he said to Him, o my lord, how can I save Israel? Indeed, my clan is the weakest in Manasseh, and I am the least in my father's house.*
>
> *And the Lord said to him surely, I will be with you, and you shall defeat the Midianites as one man.* (Judges 6:14 – 16.)

This was God telling Gideon, "You are not defined by your family, tribe, skin colour, background and position in your family". Gideon was thinking his identity was the same as that of his family. Today, a lot of people do the same in trying to define who they are. Gideon's identity was that of a mighty man, but he saw himself small because of where he was coming from. When Gideon saw himself the way God saw him, he went on to deliver the Israelites from their enemies as one man.

> *Phillip found Nathaniel and said to him, we have found him of whom Moses in the law and the prophets wrote, Jesus of Nazareth, the Son of Joseph.*

And Nathaniel said to him, "can anything good come out of Nazareth? Phillip said to him "come and see and Jesus saw Nathaniel coming towards Him and said of Him behold an Israelite indeed, in whom is no deceit. (John 1:45- 47)

Nathaniel defined who Jesus was by His origin and where he was coming from, and rightly so because it was documented in history that Nazareth is one of the lowliest places on earth. Nothing good could come out of it. Your tribe may be the smallest tribe in your village and country, but that does not make you the smallest person in life. I am from Bassa-nge in Kogi state Nigeria. Bassa-nge is the smallest tribe in Kogi state and probably one of the smallest tribes in Nigeria but that does not define me at all.

3. WHO YOU ARE IS NOT WHERE YOU WERE BORN OR HOW YOU WERE BORN

Who you are is not about where you were born and how you were born; it is why you were born that is important. Since you can't control how you were born, how and where you were born are not your identity. You were planned by God. There are no illegitimate children, you were planned by God.

Just as [in love] He chose us in Christ [selected us for Himself as His own] before the foundation of the world so that we would be Holy [that is consecrated for Him, purpose driven] and blameless in His sight in love. Ephesians 1:4 (AMP)

You did not get to choose how and where you were born, so, all that cannot define who you are. Whatever the circumstances surrounding your birth, it cannot alter God's purpose for your life.

4. YOU ARE NOT THE OPINION OF OTHERS

Proverb 29:25 (GNT) says:

It is dangerous to be concerned with what other people think of you, but if you trust the Lord, you are safe.

This is to let you know that you are not what others conclude and say about you. Don't let people's opinion form your identity. Don't let who you are be based on what family, friends and society decide for you.

Refuse to accept any opinion about you that is not consistent with God's Word. Don't let the devil attack you by making you believe you are not who God created you to be. Refuse to think you are less than who God created you to be. Following the opinion of others over God's opinion will lead you to a false identity.

You are not here to impress others. Roy T. Benneth captures it better when he said, "*You were not born on earth to please anyone; you must live life to express yourself, not to impress someone. Don't pretend to be someone you're not, and never lose yourself in search of other people's acceptance and approval.*" It is important that who you are is not determined externally by the opinions of others.

5. YOU ARE NOT HOW MUCH MONEY YOU HAVE OR HAVE ACCUMULATED

Stop defining yourself by how much money you have. A man's life does not consist of the abundance of his possessions. **Luke 12:15 "Take heed, beware of covetousness, for one's life does not consist in the abundance of his possession."** This is not poverty mentality but knowing what God truly considers you to be. Don't let how much money you have or don't have determine the value of your life. Living true to your identity is superior to how much money you have even though society has convinced many of us that wealth is the true definition of who a person is. Chasing money as your identity will cause you to lose your identity. Don't be a slave to money. Your identity is priceless.

6. YOU ARE NOT YOUR PAST

Don't let your past define you. **Isaiah 43:18 says, "Remember ye not the former things, neither consider the things of old. Behold, I will do a new thing, now it shall spring forth; shall ye not know it? I will even make a way in the wilderness and rivers in the desert."**

You will often remember your past and it would want to define who you are, but that is not your identity. The past must be buried. If you focus on past mistakes, events of the past will be replicated in the future. Both success and failure are events.

> *But all that heard him were amazed and said, is not this he that destroyed them which called on this name in Jerusalem, and came hither for that intent that he*

might bring them bound unto the chief priest. (Acts 9: 21)

Paul did not let his past define him. He became one of the biggest examples of men who did not allow their past to define them.

Your mistakes don't define you. Live your life based on vision and not your revision. Your past cannot define your future. Your past cannot stop you.

7. WHO YOU ARE IS NOT THE RELATIONSHIPS YOU HAVE OR HOW YOU WERE TREATED

What people do to you and how they treat you does not define you. Maybe you were treated poorly or neglected. People may hold negative things about you, but that is not who you are. The injustice you have suffered does not define you. Don't allow external circumstances to define you. Don't let the value of your life be based on people's evaluation or your work. Don't let how others treat you determine your identity.

8. YOU ARE NOT THE FALSE BELIEFS YOU HAVE

Don't let the devil attack you by making you believe that you are not who God created you to be. Refuse to think and believe you are less than who God created you to be. Those strongholds and lies are not who you are.

9. YOU ARE NOT THE VOCATIONS THAT OCCUPY MUCH OF YOUR LIFE (YOU ARE NOT YOUR JOB)

You exist before your job, so you are not your job. Your life continues after retirement from your job. Spending time and energy pursuing a career can cause you to feel like it is what defines you. Stop defining yourself by the job you do. The true definition of your life is not a job. You are not the job you do or the title of the job you do. The true definition of your life is not by your job.

10. YOU ARE NOT WHO THE DEVIL SAYS YOU ARE

> *Ye are of your father the devil, and the lust of your father ye will do. He was a murderer from the beginning, and abode not in the truth because there is no truth in him. When he speaketh a lie, he speaks of his own; for he is a liar, and the father of it.* (John 8: 44)

Satan has declared war on our identity perhaps because he knows that to be the surest way to wreck the relationship between us and God. Satan wants a counterfeit identity for you; so, don't believe his lies. Everything the devil says to you is a lie to distract you from who you are. The devil wants you to struggle through life with the wrong identity. He wants you to be completely ignorant of who you are in Christ. The devil will sponsor a false identity to you to keep you in self-condemnation, self-hatred, self-rejection and self-pity. Refuse to be intimidated by the devil into accepting a false identity of who you are not.

When you cannot answer the question, "Who are you?" God is left with no option than to ask. You may say I am a medical doctor, lawyer, engineer, accountant, pastor, apostle, administrator or businessman, yet, God may be saying to you "Who are you? Is that what I created you to be?" And if you listen to your heart, you will answer these questions. Pause for a while and listen to your heart to get answers to these questions. God knows every detail of your life and He will never leave you without a witness, if you are truly His child. Romans 8:14 says:

> *For as many as are led by the Spirit of God, they are the sons of God.*

It is your right therefore to receive answers to these questions: "Who am I, Lord? What is your plan and purpose for my life?" Life is full of questions but one question every man must answer is "Who are you?" If the divine program of God for your life will see fulfillment, you must be able to answer that question. The answer to that question is a matter of discovery. You must understand that purpose is not a decision but a discovery; a discovery of what you are created to be. You were created to fulfil God's purpose, and you must discover it. This is where many people miss it, they want destiny to just happen.

Your purpose in life is a matter of personal discovery; life itself is an adventure. All social, scientific, political, medical and economic advancements happened because of one discovery or the other. This shows that everything is a product of discovery. I have realized that the difference between impactful people and people without any impact is in the fact that while the former discover and follow the purpose of God for their lives, the latter do not know and do not care to discover God's purpose for their lives. If you must make a mark in life, you must discover that you are not created to do everything. You are created to do something specifically. You are created for a specific purpose.

Unfortunately, many are leaving their lives to chance. They live based on assumptions, common sense and logic. Your God-ordained purpose in life cannot be discovered by your family, friends or even your nation. There is who we should be, but we are not; there is what we should have done, but we haven't; there is where we should be, but we haven't, and it is all because we are yet to make the discovery. Becoming a person of purpose is becoming a person of discoveries. Discovering God's purpose for your life is a lifetime assignment. You discover your purpose in phases. If you want to fulfil God's purpose for your life, you must be diligent to pay the price to discover it in all the phases of your life.

Discovering God's plan for your life should be your utmost priority all the time. You must run to God always to get His plans for your life. What matters most in life is to discover and follow God's plan for your life. God wants you to discover that purpose by absolutely depending on Him to help you discover it. Many people live their lives seeking how to make money, get degrees, get married, have children, and are never really bothered with the discovery of God's purpose for their lives. You should only ignore becoming a person of purpose the day you die. True impact in life is discovering God's purpose for your life and doing it. If you discover God's purpose for your life, you will approach it with urgency to ensure the fulfillment of that glorious destiny.

Whether you know it or not, there is a purpose waiting for you to discover. When purpose is discovered, impact and relevance in life is inevitable. The discovery of purpose is the beginning of your relevance to your generation. My desire is to create a deep hunger in you to pursue the discovery of purpose. We must understand that discovery of purpose is not discovery of ambition. Many people succeed in their ambitions and fail in becoming a person of purpose. Discovery of purpose precedes giving expression to it. No discovery, no expression.

> *And he arose that night and took two wives, his two female servants, and his eleven sons, and crossed over the ford of Jabbok. He took them, sent them over the brook and sent over what he had. Then Jacob was left alone; and a man wrestled with him until the breaking of day. Now when He saw that He did not prevail against him, He touched the socket of his hip, and the socket of Jacob's hip was out of joint as He wrestled with him. And he said, "Let me go, for the day breaks" But he said, 'I will not let you go unless you bless me!" so He said to him "what is your name? He said Jacob and He said 'your name shall no longer be called Jacob but Israel; for you have struggled with God and with men and have prevailed then Jacob asked saying "tell me your name, I pray, and He said "why is it that you ask me about my name? And He blessed him there. So, Jacob called the name of place Peniel "for I have seen God face to face and my life is preserved* (Genesis

32:22 – 30 NKJV)

Life is full of questions but the most important is: "Who are you?" You don't decide who you are. Who you are has been determined before you were born. You cannot decide who you are by yourself, you can only discover who you are from your Creator. Who you are is not your decision but your discovery. Hosea 6:3a says:

Then shall we know, if we follow on to know the Lord.

One of the helps you can get from God is the timely discovery of your purpose for life. Jacob enjoyed that help from God. The discovery of purpose is a journey.

...and Jacob was left alone.

Nobody can discover your purpose for you. You don't have a similar purpose with any member of your family and that is why when it comes to the matter of discovering God's purpose for your life, you must be left alone. No one else has the right to know your destiny; that right is exclusively yours. Many people have not been left alone; no wonder it is difficult for them to discover God's plan for their lives. They are always seeking the opinion of the world to decide what to do with their lives. Societies and circumstances decide their lives for them. Don't let your life choices be based on the desires of others. Don't let them be based on popular opinions, ego or tribe. Life is discarded on the altar of popular happenings and acceptable standards of this world. To discover your life assignment, isolate yourself from the noise and voices of this world. If you are not alone, these voices will silence you from following God's plan for your life. 1 Corinthians 14:10 say:

> *There are, it may be, so many kinds of voices in the world and none of them without signification.*

God is saying for a man to discover his true destiny in Christ, he must silence every other voice and noise that hinder him from hearing from God. It is in those moments of silence and isolation that we discover God's best for our lives.

> *...and there wrestled a man with him until daybreak.*

Why did a man wrestle with Jacob all night? Jacob refused to give up his life ambitions and plans. The reason why many have not discovered the plan of God for their lives is because of their strong personal will, personal ambitions, and personal aspirations. If you must become a person of purpose, you must let go of your ways. Stop struggling with God over your own will and desires for your life. For you to discover God's purpose for your life, you must be willing to stop wrestling with God and give up your plans. Luke 22:42 says:

> *Saying, Father, if that be willing, remove this cup from me: nevertheless, not my will but thine be done.*

Notice Jesus did not struggle or fight God over His will. He was willing to do God's will. Kathryn Kulman once said, "It is very easy to be led by God if you have no choice in the matter." When you leave your choices to follow God's plan, you are on the pathway of becoming a person of purpose. You must trust God with your life and that He is able to do well with your life. Jacob had a lot of idols in his heart. He refused to let go of the things he held onto. He wanted to continue with his own plans and agenda for his life. Before you can discover and fulfil God's purpose for your life, you must give up your personal desires and trust for His plans.

> *Trust in the Lord with all your heart; do not depend on your own understanding. Seek his will in all you do, and he will show you which path to take.* (Proverbs 3:5–6 – NLT).

In becoming a person of purpose, you must practice absolute dependence. Don't be addicted to your plans. Be willing to follow God's direction for your life. Always act in a divine direction. Stop struggling with God, stop wrestling with God over His divine agenda for your life. Do you already have your plans? Seek His will and submit your plans to Him.

Some people have not discovered the purpose of God for their lives because of some character deficiencies which they are not ready to let go of. God may need to wrestle some things out of your life if you are to become a person of purpose. To discover your purpose, God Himself must deal with some things that hinder you through the renewal of your mind by His word. If you continue to oblige the flesh, you will not become all that God created you to be.

> *...Let me go, for the day breaks*

Jacob refused to let the man go until he (Jacob) discovered God's purpose for his life. In the same way, you should not stop asking God to unveil His plans to you always. You need to always ask

God to reveal His plans to you. I can imagine Jacob saying, "No! Until I discover my purpose, I will not let you go." Jacob had failed in all his man-made efforts to fulfil destiny. A lot of people today are like Jacob. Some people are in businesses where cheating people to make money is the order of the day. It is never the purpose of God for you to cut corners to succeed. Like Jacob, you need to ask for the help of the Holy Spirit, until you become all that God created you to be.

WHAT IS YOUR NAME?

God asked Jacob this question to know how Jacob saw himself, with the eyes of purpose or the eyes of circumstances. The question, "What is your name?" is the same as "Who are you?" In the school of purpose, asking questions is an important part of becoming all that God created you for.

Jacob had always thought he was created to be Jacob. He had always seen himself as Jacob, no wonder he kept struggling, lying and cheating to become a success in life. Anytime a man finds himself in such a situation, he needs to reexamine his ways. It is likely that such a man is not in the purpose of God for his life. It is your identity that determines destiny. Until you discover who you are from God's perspective, you are likely to become somebody different from what God created you to be. Who are you? What are you on earth to do? What is your life mission and purpose? Like Jacob, you may have been answering this question wrongly. Jacob answered and said, "My name is Jacob." This was a man who was created to be Israel, yet he was calling himself Jacob. Jacob was not aware or had not discovered he was created to be Israel (a nation).

Jacob struggled through life being something else other than Israel.

Other people's achievements threatened Jacob. He was easily intimidated by the success of others because he was not in God's purpose. He was always in competition with men because he did not understand his purpose. He competed with his brother, uncle and every other person around. He even competed for a wife that was not meant for him. These are the struggles of a man not walking in purpose. Circumstances and situations of life control a man who does not know his identity. If you are purposeless, you are living a high-risk life. A lot of people on earth today don't really know what they want out of life and so they don't really know what to go for. They are left at the mercy of situations and circumstances.

One of the major disasters today is that men live their lives fulfilling different purposes other than God's purpose for their lives. It does not matter whether you are a pastor or preacher, you may still be working outside the confinement of God's plan for your life. Jacob was created to be Israel, but he was living and operating like Jacob. What a tragedy! The best place to be is in the center of God's will for your life. Like we discussed in Chapter One, most people live their lives trying to survive. Survival is never the reason for life. The greatest tragedy in life is not just death but dying without fulfilling purpose. Life is not worth living when there is no purpose for living. The greatest men on earth today are men who understand God's purpose for their lives, and they make things happen at the frequency of a lifestyle of purpose and impact. If you live without discovering God's purpose for your life, your destiny is uncertain, and your future is in doubt.

You may be walking outside God's purpose for your life now,

but you can still discover and fulfil God's purpose for your life. Apostle Paul started on the wrong path of purpose. However, immediately he discovered the exact purpose of God for his life, he did not disobey. He accepted and followed God's path. He had a beautiful testimony of himself at the close of his life. He said, "I have finished my course." He had once persecuted the church, and tried to destroy it, but after he met Christ on the way to Damascus, Paul's life was changed, and he became a man that lived for the eternal purpose of God for his life.

Your life is too short to be spent being something that God did not create you to be. Your success in life is based on running on the track God gave you. To do something else is to be a failure. No matter how successful a person is, if he is not in the purpose of God, he is a failure. God's commitment to your life is to the extent to which you are committed to pursuing His purpose for your life. Until you know your identity in God, you may not like where you would eventually arrive in your journey of destiny.

> *For I know from where I came, and where I go.* (John 8:14)

Jesus knew clearly what He came to this world to do. He was not in doubt of it, and until His death on the cross, He never lost sight of His mission on earth. Knowing your purpose often starts by discovering what is not your purpose. Becoming a person of purpose implies that you are not bothered by what you have discovered you cannot do. You focus all your energy on what you have discovered you can do. God knew what He created us to be and all He is demanding from us is for us to see what He has created us to be. T.L. Osborn said, "Success in life is finding out what God is doing and doing it with Him."

> *You were there while I was being formed in utter seclusion! You saw me before I was born and scheduled each day of my life before I began to breathe. Every day was recorded in your book.*
>
> *Psalm 139:15-16 NLT*

God is the reason behind your creation, He was the one that designed you. He started your creation from His mind. He never creates anything without having something in mind. It is often said that necessity is the mother of invention. You were necessary, that is why God created you. There is an eternal purpose and divine agenda because God created you.

The world is usually led by men of strong purpose. Until you are in the purpose of God for your life, nobody will see sense in whatever you are doing because God is not seeing any sense in what you are doing. It is useless doing what you were not created to do. God does not back anything that is outside His will. You must search for the mind of God for your life. Until you see into the mind of God and get His picture for your life, you are not living this life for relevance but for irrelevance.

Living for a purpose is all about receiving a mandate, and God is the giver of the mandate. To know, you must know God. There is no other way. Rick Warren said, "Without God, life has no purpose and without purpose life has no meaning. Without meaning, life has no significance or hope." Purpose begins with God. God's purpose for your life is His will for your life, and you cannot fulfil the will of

God if you don't know God. God does not commit His will to those who do not know him. To become a person of purpose who can hear, understand and follow the voice of God, you must know God.

Are you ready to do the will of God? Are you ready to fulfil God's purpose for your life? Until you are ready and willing to do His will, God will not be quick to make known His will to you. To live outside God's purpose is to live in the wilderness. Some people are presently equating the will of God with whatsoever that is succeeding. To them, once a man is successful in the eyes of men, he is successful in the eyes of God. Real success, however, is only from God's perspective. Real success is the discovery and fulfillment of that which is God's plan for your life. Success is living and walking with the divine plan of God for your life. Some people who currently appear successful and celebrated by men may not be celebrated by God. I read this somewhere and it says, "There are two kinds of people, those who say to God, 'Thy will be done', and those to whom God says, 'All right then, have it your way.'" Where do you belong?

I like what Father Berbard O.F.M once said: "Christ put you here for a purpose known to Him. He has some work for you to discover." You have a destiny; you have a future, and God wants you to discover it. God wants you to go on a search and make a discovery. God wants you to find out His purpose for your life. God is ready and always ready to unveil it to you. You must seek to discover His purpose; your life depends on it. Proverbs 25:2 says, "It is the glory of God to conceal a thing: but the honor of kings is to search out a matter."

Take a moment

Think about what you are presently doing with your life, and search thoroughly through the help of God. Is this God's purpose for my life? Is this God's plan for my life? Now if you discover it is not God's purpose for your life, ask Him what He wants you to do and how you should go about doing what He has asked you to do.

BECOMING A PERSON OF PURPOSE

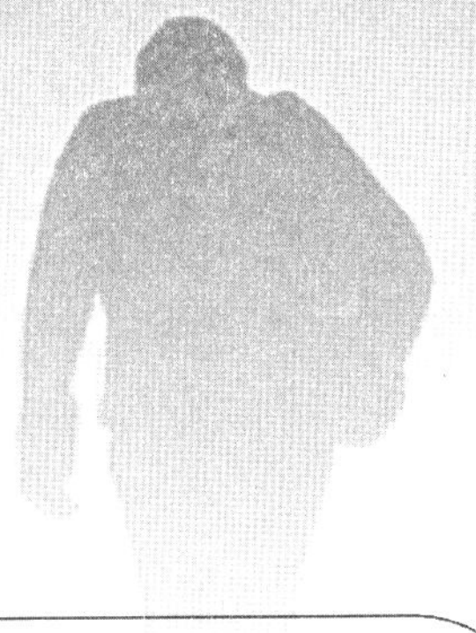

CHAPTER THREE

THE BENEFITS OF BECOMING A PERSON OF PURPOSE

Living a life of purpose is powerful and has benefits. For following God's agenda for their lives, men of purpose enjoy some divine benefits. The best of God is available for men and women of purpose. Living a life of purpose makes all the difference in the world. Living a purposeful life is advantageous and is therefore to your benefit. If you can discover and fulfil God's purpose for your life, I can assure you, you have made it in life.

Why do you need to live your life with purpose? You may think you are just okay living without a purpose, but I like you to know that there are lots of benefits to living a life of purpose. Let's consider some benefits; after all, why should anyone bother to live a life of purpose if there are no benefits to it.

BENEFIT #1: PURPOSE GIVES YOU DIRECTION IN LIFE

When you know your purpose, it gives you direction in life. It gives meaning to your existence. You cannot be a person of purpose and not know where you are headed in life. A person of purpose always enjoys direction and knows where he is going in life.

For I know where I come and where I go. John 8:15

A person of purpose knows where to go. Life is not an experiment, neither is it a gamble. A person of purpose is aware of the reason for his existence. People who live a life of purpose have limitless access to divine leading and direction. Divine direction is guaranteed when divine purpose is followed. People who know their purpose always know what to do. They are clear about what direction their lives are headed in. Living a life of purpose is that shining light that will guide you through all the seasons of your life.

Purpose makes it easy for you to know the right steps to take in life. You know what to do at the right time and in the right place. You cannot be purposeful and clueless at the same time. When people lack direction they pursue aimless things in life, but there is no hit and miss for a man of purpose. In fact, in the words of Dr Paul Enenche, such a man is "a target specific missile." Stay connected to your assignment; sooner or later men will seek to stay connected to you.

Where life is without a bearing it becomes directionless. People without direction are the biggest challenge of our generation today. You can never amount to anything great in life if you lack direction. You will arrive nowhere and go nowhere. Dr Paul Enenche wrote, "The knowledge of your purpose is the fastest route to your destination." A man of purpose knows where he is going to and what he wants in life. Men of purpose do not run in all directions. Dr John

Akpami captured it better when he said, "Those who don't know what they want end up getting what they don't want." This cannot be the case of a man of purpose. Seneca added by saying, "For a man who knows not what harbor he seeks, any wind is the right direction."

BENEFIT #2: PURPOSE GIVES YOU FOCUS AND SPEED IN LIFE

When you know your life's purpose, it becomes easier to focus on what matters the most in your life. It keeps you in the pursuit of those things that are relevant to your life and destiny, understanding purpose helps to focus and direct life's energy, time and resources to what really matters.

> *The light of the body is the eye, therefore when thine eye is single, thy whole body also is full of light; but when thine eye is evil, thy body is also full of darkness.*
> Luke 11:34

Focus gets the job done by keeping your eyes single. A purposeful person does not go about doing everything and is not easily distracted from his goals. Purpose brings focus and concentration to life. A distracted life is a purposeless life, and where there is no purpose, life is left to chance. Purposeful living equals focused living. Without purpose, other people decide life for you. You keep doing things that don't really matter to you when you are purposeless. Purpose gives focus on the right things to do; it tells you when to get things done and ensures accelerated speed in life.

Being focused helps you achieve the best God has for you. However, only purpose driven people enjoy this benefit of being focused. Staying focused comes because of knowing God's purpose for your life. When you truly know your life's purpose, you enjoy the benefits of being focused always, because you learn to give attention to the things that matter most to you. 1 Cor. 9:26 says:

> *So, I run straight to the goal with purpose in every step. I fight to win. I am not just shadow boxing or playing around.*

A man of purpose does not just play around, he goes for what is relevant to God and to his generation. Dr. John Akpami wrote, "If you have nothing pulling you forward, you will succumb to the forces pulling you backward." Purpose is the force pulling you forward in life by giving you speed. Following God's plan will ultimately guarantee you speedy fulfillment of destiny, because you have divine direction.

BENEFIT#3: PURPOSE GIVES YOU STRENGTH

One of the sure benefits of walking for a divine purpose is the fact that life becomes effortless and without stress. Life becomes a hobby to a man who is in the purpose of God for his life. When a man is walking in divine purpose, there would be enough supply of strength requisite to the fulfillment of his destiny. Such men cannot be devoid of energy. Paul, the apostle, was a man that understood the purpose of God for his life. No wonder in Philippians 4:13 he said:

I can do all things through Christ who strengthens me.

If you stay within the divine agenda of God for your life, He will strengthen you for the fulfillment of your assignment and destiny. When a man is in the divine purpose of God for his life, he receives strength to do what he has been called to do and wants to do it again and again. Such a man will discover that he is strengthened easily to do his assignment. Anytime a man discovers his destiny and purpose for living, energy becomes automatically supplied to him. David was a man that enjoyed the benefit of a purposeful life.

> *The Lord is my strength and my shield; my heart trusted in Him, and I am helped therefore my heart greatly rejoiced. (Psalm 28:7)*

The Lord strengthened David because he stayed focused on the purpose of God. Look at what is said about David in 1 Samuel 16:18 "He was a skillful man in playing musical instruments, a mighty valiant man, a man of war, a man that is prudent in matters." Have you ever wondered where he got all the strength from? A life of purpose gave it to him. Where there is purpose, there is energy for its fulfillment.

Another strength that comes upon a man of purpose is strength in the inner man. Colossians 1:11 says:

> *Strengthened with all might, according to his glorious power unto all patience and long suffering with joyfulness*

There is the inherent strength that becomes available to you once you are pursuing God's agenda for your life. You are energized with inner strength. Purpose energizes you with an inner ability to be the best for God. Ephesians 3:16 says:

> *That he would grant you according to the riches of his glory, to be strengthened with might by his spirit in the inner man.*

Once you are walking in the divine purpose of God, you are automatically strengthened with this might by the Spirit of God. So, you are strengthened with the ability of the Holy Ghost to face all challenges, difficulties and circumstances of all sorts, and to come out victoriously in the fulfillment of your divine destiny. Purpose gives you the ability to work, invigorates you with strength for your assignment and makes it very easy for you to overcome adverse conditions (discouragement).

Living a life of purpose strengthens; and this strength is in all areas of your life. So that you have divine strength, mental strength, emotional strength, and physical strength. "A merry heart doeth good like medicine, but a broken spirit drieth the bones" (Proverbs 17:22).

BENEFIT #4: PURPOSE GIVES YOU TRUE FULFILLMENT IN LIFE

A life of purpose is a life of fulfillment; People of purpose enjoy life as they find true fulfillment in the direction their lives are headed. People who lack purpose endure life no matter what they possess or acquire. No wonder Alexander the Great, in his time, conquered the well-known world in his youthful age, and when there was nothing more to conquer, he became very frustrated. At the point of death, he asked people to pour on the floor all the diamonds and other precious stones and Jewels he had acquired by conquest because none of them gave him the joy and fulfillment he craved. He was void of fulfillment despite all the treasures he acquired. He lacked true fulfillment in life.

There is nothing that gives fulfillment, excitement and joy like living in God's plan for your life. People of purpose live life with what I call "existence with excitement". They enjoy what they are doing, and they get fulfillment in pursuing life. There are people making millions of dollars yet seem not to find fulfillment in their fat bank accounts. The most exciting and fulfilled people to be with are people with a purpose. Purpose gives meaning to life.

True joy and happiness in life are a product of purpose. Dr. David Yonngi Cho captures it very well when he said, "The right kind of purpose in life is an important component in the firm foundation for stable happiness." A life without direction is the life of a vagabond. Where there is no true purpose, there can be no true happiness. The fulfillment that comes from living a life of purpose keeps pushing you to impact more lives and make a difference in your generation.

Life will be full of struggles and pains without purpose. You will never know true happiness, joy and excitement without living life for a cause. Living life for a cause is the cause of joy and fulfillment in life.

BENEFIT #5: PURPOSE GIVES HOPE

When a man walks in divine purpose, he is sure that he is not running alone; the Almighty God is with him. He is not fighting a lost battle because he has hope that he is heading somewhere. A man who does not walk in divine purpose is not only hopeless but also frustrated. A life of purpose keeps you hopeful. You cannot cause a change or make significant impact in your generation if the ingredient of hope is absent from your life.

When the troubles, difficulties and challenges of life start threatening a man, the only thing that can keep him going is hope. Hear what Job said in Job 13:15 (NIV) "Slay me, yet I will hope in Him." A man that understands and knows the purpose of God is aware that there are many battles on his way to the fulfillment of destiny, but he is also aware that the reason for the battle is the mantle. He is aware that the reason for the fight is because of the flight. Men of purpose do not give up in the battles of life, because of the possibilities that lie ahead of them. This gives them hope that they can see victory ahead. To them, every pain has a gain in front. They will never allow the battle to steal their mantle. In the face of impossible situations, you will see a man of purpose fight through with a rugged mentality towards the challenges of life. You just know that it is hope in the future that keeps him going. Hope makes you gather strength and move on. Hope is that ingredient that makes a man wait for the time of his manifestation. Hope is the engine that moves the vehicle of impact. Men of purpose enjoy free fuel of hope in the fulfillment of their destinies.

Many may be laughing at you for holding on to the purpose of God for your life because it doesn't make sense to them. They jeer because they do not see what you are doing as the popular thing to do; they consider it irrelevant, but hope keeps you going. The Bible says in Romans 5:5, says:

> *And hope makes not ashamed because the love of God is shred abroad in our hearts by the Holy Spirit who is given unto us.*

The purpose of God for your life is not meant to shame you but to bring you distinction in life and destiny. If you have a purpose, you have hope. You need to understand that your God-given purpose is that which he has written concerning you right from your mother's womb. I like what the bible says in Romans 15:4:

> *For whatever things were written before were written for our learning, that we through patience and comfort might have hope.*

Whatever has been written concerning you by God, you will fulfil in Jesus' name, Amen. God ordained your purpose. He does not lie. He will do exactly what He says He will do. No wonder 1 Thessalonians 5:24 says: *Faithful is He that calls you, who also will do it.*

Our God is a God of hope, Romans 15:13

> *Now the God of hope fill you with all joy and peace in believing that ye may abound in hope, through the power of the Holy Ghost.*

You will abound in hope continuously. Hope gives you staying power.

BENEFIT # 6: PURPOSE MAKES YOU HAVE VALUE FOR TIME

When you are living in the purpose of God for your life, you cease to be a time waster. When you don't know your purpose, you wouldn't know what to do with your life and when you don't know what to do with your life, you waste your life by wasting the time allocated to you on this side of eternity. Without purpose, time is meaningless; the reason for time is purpose. A person of purpose is a person who knows that value for time shows value for life. Without purpose, you have no value for time. The most time conscious people on earth are the most purposeful people.

Jesus was a man of purpose. He had a strong value for time. Hear what He said in John 9:4,

> *I must work the works of Him that sent me, while it is day. The night comes when no man can work.*

Jesus did not waste time within the space of the three and half years that He carried out His earthly ministry. He was able to complete His assignment on earth. While the purposeless is looking for what he will do with his time, the person of purpose is looking for more time. Waste of time is a waste of destiny. Men of purpose are productive men, because they have value for time. To a man of purpose, time wasted equals life wasted. People of purpose are highly intolerant of time wasters and aimless people. Dr Sam Adeyemi once said that while others are yet to discover what to do for the day, he has discovered what to do for the rest of his life.

People of purpose daily evaluate their lives by measuring how far they have gone in achieving God's plan for their lives. A person of purpose has something to do per time, because of their value for time. They are committed to a cause, and they allocate their time only to that cause. Most purposeless people waste their lives on trivial, inconsequential living. Not so for a person of purpose, he spends time on what would bring profit to God and humanity. No wonder Dr Paul Enenche said, "People of purpose and value are profit conscious."

Are you fulfilling God's purpose for your life? You will naturally value time.

BENEFIT #7: PURPOSE MAKES YOU AVOID WRONG CHOICES IN LIFE

Purpose influences the choices a man makes for his life. Vital choices in life are determined based on purpose. Most people leave their lives for luck. They marry by chance; they make friends by chance, and they pursue a career by chance. What a pitiable way to live life. People of purpose are deliberate about the choices they make in life. Purpose makes it easy for you to make choices. And to decide your priorities in life. Your destiny can be wasted on the altar of wrong choices. Wrong choices in life are a product of lack of understanding of God's purpose for one's life. Understanding purpose delivers people from wrong choices and relationships. Proverbs 13:20 says, "He that walketh with wise men shall be wise. But a companion of fools shall be destroyed."

A person who lacks purpose follows the popular trend and lives to please the expectations of men. Such a person will not achieve the best God has for him. People who live a life of purpose are not quick to call everyone their friends because it is purpose that determines their spouses, friends and associations. You make decisions based on the blueprint of God for your life. As we continue to become people of purpose, decision making becomes easier for us. Living a life of purpose increases your ability to make the right decisions. Choice empowers us to succeed or fail, and purpose assists us to make the right choices. People of purpose make choices in favor of God's purpose for their lives. The choices of purpose driven people are motivated by God's purpose. The purpose of God regulates their choices. Let purpose govern our choices. Let your assignment determine your alignment.

BENEFIT #8: PURPOSE MAKES YOU LIVE A LIFE OF DISCIPLINE

A lot of people have not succeeded in life because they lack discipline. Every man who became distinguished in life was a man of discipline. You cannot discover purpose and continue to live in indiscipline. The present is the route to the future; what you are doing today will affect where you will be tomorrow. Discipline takes you to your destiny. People of purpose understand the true value of discipline. Laziness and indolence are a common trait of purposeless people, and they are most spectators in all spheres of life. Refuse to be a spectator in the journey of life, be a person of purpose. Someone once said, "There is nothing in the world which helps a man surmount his difficulties, survive his disaster, and keeps him healthy and happy as the knowledge of a life task worthy of his devotion."

Discipline is not always pleasurable but living a life of purpose makes it a lifestyle for you. The writer of Hebrew agrees that it is not pleasurable but necessary for the fulfillment of purpose. Hebrew 12:11 (HCSB) "No discipline seems enjoyable at the time, but painful." However, a man of purpose understands that discipline is for his benefit. Discipline makes us benefit from all that purpose has to offer. Hebrew 12:10 (HCSB) "He does it for our benefit." A man of purpose is a lover of discipline as purpose helps him to live in discipline.

BENEFIT # 9: PURPOSE FUELS PURSUIT AND PERSISTENCE IN LIFE

Men of purpose do not give up easily. Purpose keeps them going. They are resolute in their pursuit of destiny. They are unstoppable. What makes a man pursue a cause with all his life? It is purpose. Once you know your purpose, nothing else matters to you. Men of purpose believe in their purpose to a point where they are totally consumed by it. No setback can stop a man of purpose. I like what the New Testament Apostle of purpose, (Paul) said in Acts 20:24. "But none of these things move me, neither count I my life dear unto myself, so that I might finish my course with joy and the ministry, which I have received of the Lord Jesus, to test, try; the gospel of the grace of God." Wow! Paul was so engrossed in the pursuit of his life purpose.

Paul had no plan B; no wonder none of the challenges that came his way moved him. Some people who lack the fuel of pursuit and persistence easily follow a plan b. Becoming a person of purpose will keep your mind and spirit fueled and rejuvenated. It will guide your pursuit in life. Purpose takes you out of the comfort zone of life. A man of purpose understands that what is not pursued cannot be possessed. Living on purpose fuels your pursuit and delivers your possession to you. Purpose motivates you to take steps and make moves in the direction of God's plan for your life. As we can see, Paul kept pursuing his vision despite the challenges. He had a purpose, and that gave him that fighting spirit. Are you wondering why you give up easily? Check if you have discovered something to live and die for. Dr John Akpami put it better when he said, "Vision will keep you alive when everything around is dying. What you see around you will eventually bow to what you see within you." A person of purpose is a persistent person.

You can be multi-talented and intelligent and yet without purpose; you have nothing to keep you going. Persistence is a rare virtue that comes with purposeful living. Calvin Coolidge put it better when he said, "Nothing in the world is more common than unsuccessful men with talent. Genius will not; unrewarded genius is almost a proverb. Education will not; the world is full of educated derelicts. Persistence and determination alone are overwhelmingly powerful."

BENEFIT #10: PURPOSE BRINGS DIVINE PROVISION, PROTECTION AND PRESERVATION

If you are following God's purpose for your life, divine prosperity is yours. Prosperity, abundance and supernatural supplies follow a man who is pursuing God's purpose for his life. Divine purpose guarantees provision. You cannot be in the purpose of God for your life and be in lack. God told Kenneth E. Hagin "If you follow the inward witness, I will make you rich." If you follow God's purpose for your life, I can assure you, He will make you rich. You will enjoy plenty if you are doing what God asks you to do. Psalm 23:1-3

> *The Lord is my shepherd; I shall not want He maketh me to lie down in green pastures. He leadeth me beside the still waters, he restoreth my soul: he leader me in the path of righteousness for his name's sake.*

It is said that every vision has a provision. Dr Myles Munroe captures it better when he said, "God makes provision for the vision he gives." "Vision" here should be used synonymously with purpose. Dr Paul Enenche once said, "The leading of God and lack don't co-exist, they are mutually exclusive and diametrically opposed."

God will certainly protect a man who is engrossed in enforcing His will. Following the purpose of God makes you God's ambassador on this earth. It guarantees your immunity and protection from all the onslaught of the devil. To be in God's purpose is to be in God's provision. Once you are in the plan of God, the plan of the devil can do you no harm.

BENEFIT #11: PURPOSE BRINGS YOU SUCCESS, CELEBRATION AND HONOUR IN LIFE

You cannot follow the purpose of God for your life and not stand out in your generation. Purpose brings excellence, and dignity in life. You become the delight of your generation when you are in God's purpose. You enjoy unlimited success every time you follow the plan of God for your life. Success, honor, celebration and dignity in life are the privileges of those who follow God's purpose and plan for their lives. You cannot seek to let your world know God through His purpose for your life and yet be unknown to your world.

God establishes you in success, honour and dignity as you establish His purpose on earth. God will make you a generational solution provider; you will provide answers to the questions of your generation and these solutions and answers will make you a shining light in your generation. Men of purpose are contributors, trailblazers, history makers, pacesetters, frontliners, world shakers and news makers in their generation.

Psalm 23:5 says, "Thou prepares a table for me in the presence of my enemies; thou anointest my head with oil; my cup runneth over." When you follow God's purpose, you end in success, celebration, honor and dignity in life. When we follow God's purpose and plan for our lives, we become a success in all we do. True success in life is recorded the moment a man begins to follow the plan of God for his life. Men of purpose are valuable to their generation. They bring value, and their generation honors and rewards them for bringing value. No wonder Dr John Akpami says "when you lose sight of your purpose, you lose value."

BENEFIT # 12: PURPOSE MAKES YOU RUN IN YOUR OWN LANE AND AVOID IMITATION

Walking in your divine purpose makes you to operate as yourself. Anytime you see a man operating in his uniqueness, you have seen a man running with God's purpose for His life. Purpose and originality are related. Purpose gives you your originality. You are different, and your world is seeking the real you, not an imitation of another man. Men of purpose learn to be themselves.

The pursuit of purpose is what turns you into a celebrity. Don't envy anybody, celebrate them and walk in your own uniqueness. Stop trying to be like your mentor. Stop trying to teach and preach like your father in the Lord. Operate in your own uniqueness. In the words of my good friend and brother, Steven Edward, "Discover your unique and authentic self". Every purpose is from God, nobody's purpose is superior to your own. Men of purpose don't allow anybody to make them feel inferior. Celebrate other people's uniqueness but donate yourself to being the original that God created you to be. Stop being a copycat. John Mason describes this better when he said, 'You were born an original, don't die a copy." It is frustrating attempting to be someone else. Imitation is a limitation. Be yourself and give expression to your real self. Joel 2:7 says:

> *They shall run like mighty men; they shall climb the wall like men of war; and they shall march everyone on his ways; and they shall not break their ranks.*

THE BENEFITS OF BECOMING A PERSON OF PURPOSE

Men of purpose run in their own lane, they are free from imitation and the desire to become someone else.

CHAPTER FOUR

REQUIREMENTS FOR BECOMING A PERSON OF PURPOSE

If we learn to understand the things necessary for creating the right atmosphere for us to become what God created us to be, we will be successful in life. Learning how to discover God's purpose for our life should be our greatest delight. Everyone desires to fulfil God's purpose for their lives, but not everyone understands what to do to discover it. Practicing the following will help you discover God's purpose for your life:

1. ATTITUDE OF ENQUIRY

Enquiry has to do with asking questions. If you must discover God's purpose for your life, you must learn to ask the right questions. Only those who ask questions are entitled to answers. God is ever ready to answer all your questions as it regards His purpose for your life. The reason why a lot of people don't know the plan of God for their lives is because they never get to ask God.

There are things God will tell us directly, and there are things we need to ask Him. When it comes to finding His purpose, always ask questions like "Lord, am I in the right direction? Lord, this is what I am thinking, is it according to your plan for my life?" To ask God questions is an indicator that you want to follow Him. When God answers your question, He answers it well. He tells you exactly what to do with your life. To discover God's purpose for your life, ask questions like Paul did in Acts 9:6a "And him trembling and astonished said Lord what will you have me to do?"

To discover God's purpose for your life, ask God directly, "What is your purpose for my life? Discovering God's purpose for your life starts with asking the right questions, and the right questions position you to receive the right answers from God. Jeremiah 6:16 says:

> *Thus said the Lord, stand ye in the ways, and see and ask for the old paths where is the good way and walk therein, and ye shall find rest for your souls. But they said, we will not walk therein.*

The best way for your life is God's purpose, and the major route to discovering God's purpose for your life is by asking Him. Asking God His purpose for your life shows that you place Him first above all things. It shows your heart for God. Asking God always for guidance and direction means you put God above everything and everybody and you are not afraid of hearing from Him.

Matthew 6:33 says, "But seek ye first the kingdom of God, and his righteousness; and all these things shall be added to you." To become what God created you to be, you must decide to seek His guidance, leadership and direction for your life and destiny. Giving priority to God by asking in prayer for His purpose for your life, guarantees that you will discover His purpose and plan for your life. Make no mistake: what God wants you to do with your life is more important than what you want to do with your life. So, refuse to do anything until you enquire and hear from Him. God's opinion must be of utmost priority to you. Refuse to step out until He answers you on what to do with your life. You can never get the best of God's plan if you refuse to seek His opinion on every matter. When you enquire and He is silent, don't act, wait for His answers.

You can never get the best of God if you don't ask Him questions. Until you ask and hear from God, you will be out of track in life. Until your purpose is birthed from the place of asking God in prayers, you will be out of order and out of touch in life and will never discover God's purpose and plan for your life. Matthew 7:7 says, "Ask, and it shall be given unto you; seek and ye shall find; knock, and it shall be opened unto you." God will keep unveiling His plan for you when you continue to ask, seek and knock. Are you asking God, or you are asking men? Are you asking God, or you are asking situations and circumstances? Don't be afraid of asking God for direction for your life and destiny. Enquiry is the doorway to discovery. Questions open the door to every answer that we seek.

2. PUT THE WORD ABOVE EVERYTHING

Everything about your life and destiny is provided for in God's Word. Everything you need to know about God's plan and purpose for your life is in God's Word. The Word of God is the will of God.

Inside the written Word of God, we get the spoken Word of God. When the written word is known, the revealed word is easy to find. The Word of God is the way of God, to know the way to go in life is to know the written Word of God. To be acquainted with the Word of God is to know the plan of God for your life. To become a person of Purpose and discover God's plan for your life, you must begin with God's Word. To find God's purpose for your life stay with God's Word. As you stay with God's Word, pay attention to the instructions God will give you as you read, study and meditate on His Word.

Jesus clearly saw His purpose captured in the Word just before He began His public ministry. Luke 4:16–21 clearly shows us that He came to fulfil the prophecies of the scripture. His life purpose and mission were fully captured as He studied the scripture, no wonder in verse 21, He said, "Today this scripture is fulfilled in your hearing." As you study and meditate on the Word of God, it will birth divine leading and directions that will usher you to God's plan and purpose for your life.

Another man that discovered God's purpose for His life by the Word of the Lord is Samuel. 1Samuel 3:21 shows us that God revealed Himself to Samuel by the Word of the Lord. Intimacy with the Word of God is the beginning of your journey towards becoming a person of purpose. The Word of God will open your eyes to God's purpose and plan for your life. Whatever plans God has for your life, He will sustain with His Word. The Word of God is a sure guide into God's purpose for our lives. Psalm 119:105 says, "Thy word is a lamp unto my feet, and a light unto my path." Psalm 119:130 also says, "The entrance of thy words giveth light; it giveth understanding unto the simple." Every time you expose yourself to God's Word you gain light insight and revelation into the mind of God for your life. The Word of God carries the light of God, and the light of God gives us direction for life and destiny.

You must learn the Word of God because the voice of God bears witness with the Word of God. God never says anything to us outside the Word of God. We can pick divine direction to discover and fulfil God's purpose for our lives from His word. To discover your purpose easily, stay with God's Word. Colossians 3:16 says, "Let the word of Christ dwell in you richly in all wisdom; teaching and admonishing one another in psalms and hymns and spiritual songs, singing with grace in your hearts to the Lord."

To discover God's purpose for your life, the Word of God must dwell in you richly. The Word of God is dwelling so poorly in you, and yet you want to discover God's purpose for your life? The Word of God contains the general and the specific will of God for our lives. Some people want to know the specific will of God concerning His purpose for their lives, yet their Bible is closed all week. To discover God's purpose and plan for your life, keep your Bible open continuously by feeding, meditating and practicing the Word.

Becoming a person of purpose is from the written Word of God. The Word of God contains the whole counsel of God for your life. Hebrew 10:7 says, "Then said I, Lo, I come in the volume of the book, it is written of me, to do the will of God." Everything about God's purpose for your life is in the written Word of God. Load yourself with Scripture in such a way that light jumps out to give you direction for life and destiny. Knowledge of God's Word is knowledge of God's purpose for your life. When you make constant contact with God's Word, you make constant contact with God's will for your life. Meditate on God's Word until it soaks your spirit. Our guide into the discovery of God's purpose is His word.

The Word of God is for my making. To be made in life is to discover and fulfil God's purpose. God will make you what he wants you to be by His Word. Joshua 1:8 says:

> *This book of the law shall not depart out of thy mouth; but thou shall meditate therein day and night, that thou mayest observe to do according to all that is written therein. For then thou shalt make thy way prosperous and then thou shall have good success.*

The Word makes you what God created you to be. Good success and impacting others are in discovering and fulfilling purpose and this can only be discovered through His Word. Failure to stay with God's Word is failure to discover purpose. You cannot ignore the Word of God and discover destiny. You can see your future from God's Word. Studying the Bible, meditating on it and praying about it helps us to gain deeper understanding of His purpose for our life. Everything in our life begins and ends with God's Word. The desire to discover God's purpose for your life will get you closer to the Bible.

Intimacy with the Word of God positions you to discover God's purpose for your life. If you stay with God's Word, you will locate His purpose and plan for your life. If you spend quality time with God's Word daily, you will never miss the purpose of God for your life. Giving the Word of God attention is how you become a person of purpose. To be serious with God's Word is to be serious in becoming a person of purpose.

3. SEEK TO GLORIFY GOD ALWAYS

God created us first and foremost to bring Him glory. We all have one purpose: to glorify God in everything we do. Seeking to glorify God is an important part of seeking to fulfil His purpose for your life. The Bible instructs us in 1 Corinthians 10:31

> *Therefore, whether you eat or drink, or whatever you do, do all to the glory of God.*

When glorifying God becomes the motive of all you do in life, you will never miss God's purpose and plan. When we get ourselves consumed with bringing glory to God, we enjoy access to His purpose and counsel. When you get preoccupied with glorifying God, you are on the path of discovering God's purpose and plan for your life. The hallmark of glorifying God is that of honouring God with one's life. Once your life is always honoring God, you will walk into His divine purpose for your life effortlessly. We are free to decide how we want to live our lives, but when you consciously decide to bring God glory and honor always, you have just signed up to know His mind concerning your life always.

Becoming a person of purpose involves making sure all our actions seek to glorify Jesus. If we seek to glorify God always in all we do, then our Father God will be always well pleased with us, and when He is pleased with us, knowing His will concerning our lives and destiny becomes easy. Stop trying to discover God's purpose and plan for your life when the matter of pleasing the Father is not a priority to you. Make glorifying God the priority of your life and you will flow in the divine purpose of God for your life effortlessly.

It is amazing how men seek self-glorification, pursue personal ambitions and give God the back seat in their lives, and yet tell you they want to know God's purpose and plan for their lives. When you don't seek to fulfil destiny, to be famous or have material possessions, but to please our Father God, I can assure you, you will never miss God's purpose and plan for your life. You are not seeking to glorify God if you are living life just for yourself. 1 Peter 4:11 says:

> *If anyone speaks, let him speak as the oracles of God. If anyone ministers, let him do it as with the ability which God supplies that in all things God may be glorified through Jesus Christ to whom belong the glory and the dominion forever and ever.* **Amen.**

If we seek to glorify God always, we are showing our worship, honor, commitment and reverence for Him. You cannot be stranded in life because by glorifying God in all you do, you will enjoy divine direction. I love how Dr. Joshua Tende captures it: "Build your life centered around glorifying Jesus, and you'll never lack the backing of the Holy Spirit." Always ask yourself, "Will this thought, word or deed glorify God?" Whenever you ask this, you gain access to directions for your life and destiny. When you seek to fulfil destiny, not for personal ambition but to please the father, you are showing commitment and passion to doing God's will when it is unveiled to you. I love this prayer in Hebrews 13:21:

> *May God, make you complete in every good work to do His will, working in you what is well pleasing in His*

sight, through Jesus Christ, to whom be glory forever and ever. Amen.

May this become your prayers always. If you understand that God's general purpose for us all is to bring Him glory, and you set out to bring Him glory, you will fulfil His purpose for your life. Our greatest desire in life is to live to give glory God. All our purpose must bring glory to God. Romans 11:36 (LB) says, "For everything comes from God alone. Everything lives by his power, and everything is for his glory." Let this be the goal of your life and you will never miss the purpose of God for your life. God's primary purpose for our lives is to bring Him pleasure. God created you to give, please and satisfy His desires and not yours. (Rev 4:11). We are formed to live for God and His pleasure. The easiest way to discover purpose is to seek to glorify God and give Him pleasure. You are custom made in heaven to glorify God; you are wired to bring glory to God.

If you are passionate about glorifying God, you will find purpose for your existence. If you get busy glorifying God, which is our primary purpose for existence, you will not miss out of your specific and secondary purpose for existence. The easiest way to discover purpose is to glorify God.

4. PASSION FOR THE WILL, PURPOSE AND PLAN OF GOD

Passion is the gateway into discovering God's purpose and plan for your life. Those who want to do God's will must have a burning desire to be in His plan always. You cannot know God's purpose for your life if you are not desperate and interested in knowing His will. Those who have strong personal wills, personal ambitions, personal aspirations; those who are egocentric and full of themselves cannot receive God's direction for their lives and destiny. When you have decided to pursue nothing except God's direction for you, you will discover God's plan and purpose all the time. When you refuse to take any step unless God directs you, you will never miss out of God's plan for your life. Your passion for the will of God determines if you will know and become all that God created you for.

One of the secrets of discovering God's purpose and plan for your life is developing unconquerable passion for God. You cannot be passionate for the will, purpose and plan of God and miss it in life. Passion for the purpose of God is a key way in always discovering and following His purpose. Jesus showed passion for the will of God in Luke 22:42 by saying

> *Father, if thou be willing, remove this cup from me; nevertheless, not my will but thine be done.*

You don't get to know the purpose of God if you are not always passionately seeking to know. You must be deeply consumed with the passion to know by continuous seeking and searching. Hosea 6:3 says, "*Then shall we know, if we follow on to know, the lord; his going is prepared as the morning and he shall come unto us as the rain, as the later and former rain to the earth.*" People of purpose let go of their ways and go in search of God's best for their lives, and they go about this search passionately and are unwilling to do anything unless they hear from God. They wait and watch out for God always. Habakkuk 2:1 captures it better by saying:

I will stand upon my watch and set me upon the tower and will watch to see what he will say unto me, and what I shall answer when I am reproved

Notice he said "...and will watch to see what he will say." That is the mindset of a person of purpose. Refusal to do anything without God's permission guarantees you access always to discovering His purpose and plan for your life. When you are passionate for the will, purpose and plan of God, you are focused only on doing what you have been instructed to by God. Once this becomes a lifestyle for you, discovering God's purpose and plans happen naturally for you. Passion for His will is a pointer to His purpose for your life. We will talk more about passion subsequently in this book. However, make sure your passion to know God's will and plan for your life is unhindered. Make sure you are not struggling for your own will but for God's purpose and agenda.

5. BE WILLING AND READY TO OBEY GOD'S INSTRUCTIONS ALWAYS

And we are his witnesses of those things; and so is also the Holy Ghost, whom God hath given to them that obey him. Acts 5:32

Our daily consecration to God must always show in our willingness to obey Him. It must show in our willingness to go wherever He wants us to go and, in our willingness, to do whatever He wants us to do. You are not created to do your own will but God's, will and to discover God's will, God must see that you are willing and ready to obey His instructions always. Willingness is being ready to yield to God's instruction always without resistance. If you continue to show willingness and readiness to obey God's instruction, then you are never going to miss out God's best for your life. The rebellious cannot discover God's plan and purpose for their lives. The plan of God is easy to know when you are willing and ready to give up your own plans. When God speaks to you and you instantly obey Him, you are showing willingness and readiness, then He will show you more.

Many people keep struggling with God's instructions in minor things, yet wonder why there are not hearing Him on major things. Learn to practice willingness and readiness to obey little instructions then you will hear God in the major things also. Jesus clearly showed His willingness and readiness to do God's will. See what He said about Himself in John 5:19, 30

> *Then answered Jesus and said unto them, verily, verily I say unto you, the son of man can nothing of himself, but what he seeth the father do, for what things soever he doeth, these also doeth the son likewise.*
>
> *I can of mine own self do nothing as I hear, I judge and my judgment is just; because I seek not mine own will, but the will of the father which hath sent me.*

You cannot be full of your own will and still locate the purpose of God for your life. When you give up your will for the will of God, purpose is birthed. Willingness and readiness to do what God says to do is what commits God to unveiling His purpose to us.

Whatever God says you should do is the route to being the best in life. It is not enough to know the will of God, but be willing and ready to do it. Passing the willingness and readiness test qualifies you for clear cut direction for the future.

Your willingness and readiness to obey instruction is seen in how promptly you obey God's instruction for your life. Obeying the initial instructions of the Holy Spirit positions you to receive the next instructions. Readiness and willingness show in your prompt response to God's instruction. Prompt obedience is of great importance. We must understand that delayed obedience is the same thing as disobedience. Our obedience to God's instruction must be prompt for us to fully become the best God created us for. Anytime you receive instructions, and you promptly respond and obey, you will always get divine directions for your life. The discovery of our God ordained purpose is tied to our willingness to do his will always. Those who obey God's Word with joy and excitement are candidates for purpose discovery. Our commitment to the will of God will show in our obedience; no wonder the Bible says in Isaiah 1:19: *"If ye be willing and obedient, ye shall eat the good of the land."*

Do you already have your plans? Are you willing and ready to let go of them for the purpose and plan of God for your life? Willingness is key to discovering God's plan for your life. Our willingness shows we believe God's purpose and plan for our life to be the best. Becoming a person of purpose shows in how desirous you are in knowing and doing the mind of God. to know the purpose of God for your life, willingness will be demanded from you. Do you desire to know the purpose of God for your life? Is your willingness commensurate to your desire? We can't scam God. He knows when we are willing and ready to obey Him. Your heart must be willing and ready to obey God's instruction always. A willing heart to obey God's instruction is a heart that will never miss God's will, purpose and plan.

6. ABSOLUTE DELIGHT AND DEPENDENCE ON THE LORD

To delight in the Lord is to be a passionate lover of God. It is to put God first in everything. It means to love God above the things of this world. Only lovers of God are entitled to fully realizing heaven's agenda for their lives and destiny. Loving the things of this world more than God is proof that you won't be interested in becoming a person of purpose. Delight in the Lord is a choice, and it is a choice people who want to become people of purpose must make. To love God above all things is not optional for a man of purpose. It is a core course in the school of destiny.

Love for God is a major key for discovering God's purpose for your life. You cannot truly love God and not discover His purpose and plans for your life. The higher your love for God, the clearer you see God's plan and purpose for your life. When you love God sincerely, you will continue to fulfil His purpose for your life. Love for God continually positions you to hear from God as regarding your life and destiny. If you are not hearing from God, check your love for Him. Intimacy with God brings revelation from God to you. The secrets of God are unveiled to lovers of God. Psalm 37:4:

Delight thyself also in the Lord; and he shall give the desire of thine heart.

Every time you show delight in the Lord, you make yourself available for Him to give you direction for life and destiny. The Psalmist also added in Psalm 25:12–14.

> *What man is he that feareth the Lord, him shall he teach the way that he shall choose. His soul shall dwell at ease; and his seed shall inherit the earth.*
>
> *The secret of the Lord is with them that fear Him, and He will show them his covenant.*

You cannot truly love God without Him revealing to you His Purpose and plans for your life. The love of God engenders the discovery of your divine destiny. Your access to the mind of God is made easy by your love for God.

Lovers of God don't struggle to access the purpose and plan of God for their lives. Many people want to know God's purpose for their lives, but they don't love and fear God. When you are in love with God, you and His purpose for your life are dear to Him. So, purpose cannot be hidden from you. My advice to you is this: if you have not discovered God's purpose for your life, just keep loving Him. Those who love God more, will access His purpose and plans more for their lives.

The Bible is full of stories of men who discovered and fulfilled God's purpose for their lives out of a burning love for God. Let me share the story of John D. Rockefeller. He was the richest man in the world in his own time; the first acknowledged American billionaire. He was a devoted Baptist who supported many church-based institutions. He was an addicted giver whose principle was based on

Luke 6:38. He taught a Sunday school class and was a church sexton. In the history of America, he is regarded as the richest of all generations. Hear what he said: "There is nothing in this world that compare with the Christian fellowship; nothing can satisfy but Christ." Becoming a person of purpose is becoming a person that loves whatever God loves with passion. It is a lifestyle where, what matters to God, matters to you.

Your love for God determines how much of His purpose for your life you will pursue. You cannot expect to fulfil God's divine purpose for your life while keeping Him outside your daily schedule. You cannot discover God's purpose for your life if love for God is not in you. Love for God gives us access to revelation. 1Cor. 2:9 says:

> *But as it is written, eye hath not seen, no ear heard, neither have entered into the heart of man the things which God hath prepared for them that love Him.*

Intimacy with God is key to fulfillment of destiny. When you love God, you "command" him to open up to you all the time. When you are consumed with God's love, your destiny will open up to you.

If you want to go far with God, stop depending on your strength and ability. Depend on Him absolutely and cooperate with Him. Whatever He tells you to do, do it. Refuse to depend on yourself. Our fulfillment of destiny depends on how much of help we receive from God. Fulfilling destiny depends on how much we depend on the Holy Spirit to help us. Absolute dependence on God is a major way to the discovery of purpose. If you depend on yourself to achieve anything in life outside God, you are a failure. When you do not depend on anything but God, you will always find out His purpose and plan for your life. Let God be the only one you depend on for your life and destiny. The best of our lives comes out from depending on God always. God shows His purpose and plans to a man who is fully dependent on Him. Without God you can do nothing—including discovering and fulfilling purpose.

Don't make the mistake of thinking you can fulfil destiny on your own. Stop deceiving yourself; you cannot do it yourself. See what Ecclesiastes 9:11 (NLT) says:

> *I have observed something else under the sun. The faster runner does not always win the race, and the strongest warrior doesn't always win the battle. The wise sometimes go hungry, and those who are educated don't always lead successful lives. It is all decided by chance, by being at the right place at the right time.*

You can only be at the right place at the right time by depending on God. A person who depends on God cannot miss his place in life. You will miss God's purpose and plans for your life, depending on anything or anybody outside of Him. Keep looking onto God. Psalm 34:5 says:

> *They looked unto him and were lightened: and their faces were not ashamed.*

You can trust God with your life. You can trust His plans for your life. He has your best interest at heart. It was Dr Simon Daramola that said, "Before you leave God's will for your life, be sure you can do for yourself more than what God can do for you." To fulfil God's purpose for your life, you must practice absolute dependence and carry the mentality of Bishop David Oyedepo, who once said, "Whatever God cannot do, let it remain undone." When you lose God's backing, you become nothing. Your future is not in your plan but God's plan. If you want to secure your future, depend on God absolutely.

7. ATTITUDE OF MEEKNESS, PATIENCE AND QUIETNESS

The attitude of meekness is coming to God with the attitude of nothingness. It is leaving behind all you know and have achieved when you come to God. Meekness is coming to God ready to do anything He says and being ready to be taught by Him on how to discover and fulfil destiny. Meekness equals *teacheability*. Anytime you go to God with the attitude of a big man who knows what to do, you are not ready for His best for your life. Meekness before God attracts His divine guidance and direction. It takes meekness to truly fulfil God's plan and purpose for your life. Psalm 25:9 says:

> *The meek will he guide in Judgement: and the meek will he teach his testimonies.*

The virtue of meekness before God is one key that triggers the right atmosphere for the discovery of purpose. Behind every great destiny we have seen in God for our generation, is the attitude of meekness in approaching God. Becoming a person of purpose is becoming a person who accepts imperfection of his own purpose and plan and looks up to God only. If you must discover God's purpose for your life, you must embrace meekness. The desire to go before God to find out His purpose is a virtue of meekness. The person of purpose must be willing to be corrected by God when he misses it. He must be willing to accept where he missed it and be ready to change plans to align with God's agenda. Jesus said in Matthew 11:29,

> *Take my yoke upon you and learn of me; for I am meek and lowly in heart; and ye shall find rest unto your souls.*

Jesus is our perfect example of a man of purpose. He embraced the virtue of meekness, and He is asking us to do the same. The capacity of meekness determines the capacity of your hearing from God to fulfil destiny. To discover God's plan for your life, don't be consumed with your own plans. Be humble enough to look foolish before men to do what God has asked you to do. Ignoring what men think or say is an attitude of meekness. Bishop David Oyedepo said, "When people are mocking you, God is busy making you."

The reason why most people have not discovered God's purpose for their lives is that they are too much in a hurry to see things happen. When your spirit is too much in a haste to get things done, it is a sign that you lack meekness. Don't ever force yourself into doing anything without hearing from God. Learn to wait for His guidance. Don't force yourself out of God's purpose for your life by being in a haste always. People that live in anxiousness and anxiety make it difficult for themselves to access God's plan and purpose for their lives. Becoming a person of purpose is becoming a person who does not fret, but who is ready to wait for God's instructions.

Impatience in following and hearing God's voice is the ruin of destiny. Trying to go outside of God's timing is disaster.

To understand the purpose of God, you must understand the timetable of God. If you are a patient person, you will not try to make things happen by yourself. Patience is the ability to wait for God, no matter the situation, no matter the delays, challenges or difficulties. Impatience will make you seek plan B and alternatives to God's purpose and plan for your life. Impatience is the reason why people settle for what is not God's plan for their lives. James 1:4 says:

> *But let patience have her perfect works that you may be perfect and entire, wanting nothing.*

The patience to wait for the unfolding of God's plan is a great key in getting the best of God. God keeps to timing, always wait for His timing. The reason why people miss out of God's program for their lives is due to their observation on timing.

> *But when the fullness of the time was come, God sent forth his son, made of a woman, made under the law.*
> Galatians 4:4

I have realized that when a man lacks the virtue of patience, he misses his timings, and it may take years to recover those divine timings. To become a person of purpose, a man must understand the waiting process. A person of purpose is patient with God no matter how long it takes, he is ready to wait for the plan of God to unfold, no matter how long. A person of purpose knows it is either God or God. Becoming a person of purpose is becoming a person who refuses to organize a plan B for God. A person who can handle any delay can certainly handle discovering and fulfilling God's purpose and plan for their lives. A person of purpose who desires to discover and fulfil purpose will never give up on the pursuit of divine agenda. The person of purpose is that man who is ready to wait for it. Quit giving God deadlines. Impatience can cost you your life.

When God is silent, don't act; when He is quiet, don't talk. Always maintain a quiet spirit. Some people cannot access the purpose of God for their lives because they allow too much noise around them. God wants us to discover His purpose for our lives, but many times we don't live a quiet life, and this hinders getting direction from God. People who set aside time each day to just sit and listen make it easy to know and discover God's purpose and plan for their lives. We hear from God easily when we quiet our spirits to hear from Him. To discover and fulfil God's purpose for your life, you must practice quietness on the inside and outside. Those who make a habit of seeking God in stillness, silence and contemplation always get to know the mind of God. This attitude makes the discovery of purpose easy. If you want to find what atmosphere is necessary to discover God's purpose, certainly, quietness is one of them. Restlessness is a sign you are not ready to hear God's plan for your life, and it shows you don't believe God will direct you right. See what Isaiah 28:16 says:

> *Therefore, thus said the Lord God behold, I lay in Zion for a foundation a stone, a tried stone, a precious corner stone, a sure foundation: he that believeth shall not make haste.*

You must make a habit of deliberately creating time to be quiet and listen to God. This is a major platform for hearing from God, where a lot of people have discovered God's purpose and plan for their lives. If you are too busy to be quiet, you are too busy to hear from God and discover His purpose for your life. Being restless in your mind is being restless to hear from God. The quiet mode births the listening and hearing mode, and the listening and hearing mode activates the discovery of purpose mode.

> *Be still and know that I am God, I will be exalted among the nations, I will be exalted in the earth.* (Psalm 46:10)

Any time you are still, you get to know something from God. Quietness is a proof you want to hear from God. It is also a proof that you value the voice of God. It is in this period of silence and quietness that God reveals Himself to us. It is in quietness that God reveals things about His purpose and plans for our lives. Jesus made it an attitude to seek God in quietness always. See Mark 1:35:

> *Very early in the morning while it was still dark, Jesus got up, left the house and went off to a solitary place, where he prayed.*

Get comfortable with creating quiet times to hear from God. If you want to hear God, then silence all the noises around your life. Sometimes, like Jesus, go to a solitary place. Let this become a habit. Oswald Chambers writes, "Get into the habit of saying "Speak Lord" and life will become a romance." If God will speak to you, you must be quiet to hear Him.

8. BE CONSUMED WITH THE DESIRE TO EXTEND THE FRONTIERS OF GOD'S KINGDOM

There are depths in God that you will never know until you begin to be consumed with the desire to expand God's kingdom on earth. Too many people want to discover God's purpose and plan for their lives while kingdom expansion is secondary to them. Commitment to expanding God's kingdom on earth is committing yourself to receiving directions regarding your own life and destiny. Any time you see a man pursuing kingdom agenda, you have seen a man who will not miss out of God's purpose and plans for his life. If extending the frontiers of God's kingdom is your burden, the discovery of God's plan and purpose becomes easy. God leads men into that which will expand His kingdom on earth.

If you want God's purpose and plan to become clearer to you, get busy with extending God's kingdom around you. Every time a man gives himself to expanding God's kingdom, he is opening himself to hearing more from God as regards his life and destiny.

> *Cry yet, saying, thus saith the Lord of Hosts, my cities through prosperity shall spread abroad, and the Lord shall comfort Zion, and yet choose Jerusalem.* (Zachariah 1:17.)

As God's children, our topmost priority is to spread the kingdom of God on earth. When you face kingdom expansion, destiny discovery and fulfillment become easy. One way to extend the frontiers of God's kingdom is through the spread of the gospel. Every time you promote the spread of the gospel, you get yourself to discover and fulfil God's purpose and plan. If we get committed to the spread of the gospel, we will never lack God's direction in other areas of our lives. Dr Joshua Tende captures it very well when he said, "When you focus on the spread of the gospel, you are amplifying the voice of the Holy Spirit in your heart." Spreading the gospel is a sure way of ensuring that you receive clear direction for life and destiny. To be outstanding in following God's plan for you, you must be outstanding in promoting the agenda of God in all you do.

Saturate your life with the desire to bring Christ to your generation. The primary purpose of the church of Christ on earth is the spread of the gospel, and you cannot be engaged in this primary purpose of the church and miss out of God's primary purpose for your life and destiny. To be committed to the spread of the gospel gives God delight. The spread of the gospel is a primary concern to God. Hear what Jesus said in Luke 19:10:

> *For the son of man is come to seek and to save that which was lost.*

This shows that God is passionate about the spread of the gospel. Are you passionate about the spread of the gospel? You cannot be passionate about the spread of the gospel and amount to nothing in life. The urgency of the spread of the gospel was emphasized by Jesus in Mathew 9:38. It says:

> *Pray ye therefore the Lord of the harvest, that He will send forth labourers into His harvest.*

Mark 16:15 *And he said unto them, go ye into all the world, and preach the gospel to every creature.*

The spread of the gospel is the heartbeat of God, and He has passed the responsibility of spreading the gospel to us. We are co-labourers with God today in spreading the gospel. 1 Corinthians 3:9 says, "For we are labourers together with God. Ye are God's husbandry, ye are God's building."

There are depths in God's purpose and plans for your life that you will not know until you get yourself busy with the spread of the gospel. Spread of the gospel is the priority of God and once your priority is same with the priority of God, you will never miss His plans for your life. The spread of the gospel gives God joy. Therefore, to experience joy in your own life and destiny, continuously give God joy through the spread of the gospel. The spread of the gospel brings honor to God, and it will certainly bring honor to you.

The spread of the gospel is a concern to God. Hear what Jesus said to Kenneth E. Hagin about the spread of the gospel. Rev. Hagin was ministering in Rockwall Texas in 1950 and had an open vision in which Jesus spoke to him about being a soul winner.

Jesus was standing there, and I stood in His presence. He was holding a crown in His hands. This crown was so extraordinarily beautiful that human language cannot begin to describe it." Jesus told me, "This is the soul winner's crown. My people are careless and indifferent. This crown is for every one of my children… But my people are too busy, they put it off, and souls are lost because they will not obey me.

Jesus said that people selfishly say they are ready for heaven.

They talk about mansions and the glories of heaven while many around them live in darkness and hopelessness. Jesus said I should share my hope with them and invite them to come to Heaven with me.

Then Jesus turned to me and said, "Now let us go down to hell" ...we went down to hell, and as we went into that place, I saw what appeared to be human beings wrapped in flames... Jesus told me "Warn men and women about this place" and I cried out with tears that I would."

To know the passion of God is to know your purpose on earth. Get busy with soul winning and you will never miss out of God's purpose and plan for your life.

9. MINISTERING TO THE LORD ALWAYS

Ministering to the Lord in thanksgiving, praise and worship creates an atmosphere conducive for hearing from God as it regards His purpose and plan for our lives. Ministering to the Lord in thanksgiving, praise and worship makes divine guidance and direction easy. Once we worship, praise and thank God as a lifestyle, we position ourselves to receive direction for our lives and destinies. Worshipping, praising and thanking God makes our lives to bring sweet aroma to the Father. It is pleasing the Father in all ramifications. Learn to always magnify, exalt and glorify the name of Jesus. Doing this puts you in position to discover and fulfil God's purpose for your life.

> *Now there were in the church that was at Antioch certain prophets and teachers as Barnabas and*

Simeon that was called Niger and Lucius of Cyrene and Manaen which had been brought up with Herod the Tetrarch and Saul. As they ministered to the Lord, and fasted, the Holy Ghost said, separate me Barnabas and Saul for the work whereunto I have called them. (Acts 13:1-2)

Notice that it was while they ministered to the Lord and fasted that the Holy Ghost said, "Separate me Barnabas and Saul" and handed them vital instruction for their ministries. When you create the atmosphere of ministering to the Lord in praise, worship and thanksgiving, you walk in the light of direction for your life and destiny. The direction and guidance of destiny travels in an atmosphere of joy and excitement. See what Isaiah 30:29 – 30 says:

Ye shall have a song, as in the night when a holy solemnity is kept; and gladness of heart as when one goeth with a pipe to come unto the mountain of the Lord, to the mighty one of Israel.

And the Lord shall cause his glorious voice to be heard and shall show lighting down of his arm with the indignation of his anger and the flame of devouring fire, with scattering and tempest and hartstones.

To live a lifestyle of praise, worship and thanksgiving is to hear God easily for directions to fulfill your life's purpose and assignment. To live in sadness, frustration and depression is to make it difficult to hear from God. However, living in joy and excitement by ministering to the Lord in praise, worship and thanksgiving positions you become a person of purpose. Psalm 89:15 says, "Blessed is the people that know the joyful sound: they shall walk, O Lord in the light of your countenance". This clearly shows that there is a connection between ministering to the Lord and the voice of the Lord for guidance for destiny fulfillment. It is not hard to receive direction for destiny, if ministering to the Lord in praise, worship and thanksgiving is intact.

In spending time in praise, thanksgiving and worship, we learn the voice of God. When we learn the voice of God, His purpose becomes our natural habitat. The objective of praise, worship and thanksgiving in this case is to help you become familiar with the voice of God. Becoming familiar with the voice of God is becoming a person of purpose. My advice to you is to develop in ministering to the Lord, so that you may hear from Him, and when you hear from Him, He will unveil his plan and purpose to you.

10. GIVE ATTENTION TO YOUR MENTORS

Many times, when we listen to our mentors speak, especially on what they see and notice in our lives, it gives us a clue to what God's purpose and plan for our lives are. By consistently listening to your mentors, you get directions necessary for life and destiny. Make it an attitude to pay attention to the teachings and instructions of your mentors. Listening to your mentors will enhance your ability to discern the voice of God clearly. Isaiah 30:20-21 says:

> *And though the Lord give you, the bread of adversity and the order of affliction, yet shall not thy teachers be removed into a corner anymore, but thine eyes shall*

see thy teachers; and thine ears shall hear a word behind thee, saying, this is the way, walk in it, when you turn to the right hand and when ye turn to the left.

To ignore mentors or mentorship is to ignore one important key for the discovery of God's purpose and plans for your life. Timothy, in the Bible got clear cut direction on following God's plan for his life by paying attention to the counsels that Paul, his mentor offered to him. If you are missing God's plan and purpose for your life, mentors will guide you in the right direction. A trusted mentor will not lead you astray.

A mentor, most times, can see your future before you do. So, their instructions, corrections, guidance and counsel will help guide you in the right path for your life and destiny. A mentor can see beyond where you are. Cultivating a teachable spirit requisite to paying attention to your mentors will go a long way in accelerating your journey of becoming a person of purpose. A trusted mentor can offer advice and counsel when it comes to following God's plan for your life and these counsels are often very valuable. The value from the counsel of a mentor comes from the fact that they have walked the road before you. A mentor can guide you in the right direction and help you avoid the wrong pathway for your life and destiny. When it comes to the fulfillment of purpose, there is a vast difference between those who have been mentored, pastored or tutored, and those who have not.

11. BE CONSCIOUS OF YOUR IDENTITY IN CHRIST

You cannot be conscious of your identity in Christ if you are not born again. The first way to discover your identity in Christ is to be born again. You must first have a relationship with Jesus Christ. The source of every identity crisis is alienation from God. Being born of your parents is a natural phenomenon, but being born of God is supernatural. Being born again is a shift in your identity. You must believe in your heart and confess with your mouth; you are born again.

> *If thou shall confess with thy mouth the lord Jesus and shall believe in thine heart that God hath raised Him from the dead, thou shall be saved.* (Romans 10:9)
>
> *Therefore, if any man be in Christ, he is a new creation: old things are passed away; behold all things are become new.* (2 Corinthians 5:17)

Once you become born again, you must live in the consciousness of who you are in Christ to be able to discover and fulfill God's purpose. We are made new creatures the moment we become born again. The new birth is not what you made yourself, it is what God made you. At the new birth, your spirit was recreated and that means you are on the path to fulfilling God's purpose and plan for your life. You will fulfill God's purpose, if you walk in the consciousness of who you are in Christ, because you've got the very life and nature of God in you.

Through the new birth, you are in union with God. No room for failure in life and destiny. Not fulfilling God's purpose is not part of

God's plan for you in the new birth. One of the most important ways to know who you are and what God created you to do is to develop the consciousness and understanding of who you are in Christ. We have an identity in the spirit realm and to become a person or purpose, we must walk in the consciousness of that identity. Galatians 2:20 says:

> *I am crucified with Christ; Nevertheless, I live, yet not I, but Christ liveth in me; and the life which I now live in the flesh I live by the faith of the son of God, who loved me, and gave himself for me*

If you don't know who you are in Christ, you will never discover who you are in life.

Consciousness of your identity in Christ changes the way you think and live. And the way you think and live can affect the discovery and fulfillment of God's purpose for your life. Saturate your life with the consciousness of who you are in Christ, and you will be a big success in life and destiny.

12. DISCONNECT YOURSELF FROM PAST NEGATIVE EXPERIENCES

> *Forgetting those things that are behind, I look forward...* Philippians 3:13-14

Once you become born again, the Bible tells us that you have now become a new creation in Christ Jesus. If you will discover and fulfill the divine destiny that God has for you, you must disconnect yourself from past negative experiences. To become a person of purpose, you must learn to let your past experiences go. Some people have not been able to discover and fulfill God's purpose for their lives because of past negative experiences. To keep dwelling on past negative experiences is to stay away from discovering and fulfilling God's purpose and plan for your life. You must let your past fully go, so you can discover the divine destiny that God has set for your life.

> *But Jesus said to him, No one having put his hand to the plough, and looking back, is fit for the kingdom of God.* Luke 9:62.

Dwelling on past negative experiences makes you unfit for the discovery of God's purpose and plan for your life. no one who dwells in the past can discover God's best for his life.

13. WATCH YOUR TONGUE: BE CAREFUL WHAT YOU SAY ABOUT YOURSELF

If you are going to be a person of purpose, you must watch your tongue and be very mindful about what you say about yourself.

> *The one who guards his mouth preserves his life, the one who opens wide his lips comes to ruin.* Proverbs 13:3 (NASB)
>
> *Set a guard over my mouth, lord; keep watch over the door of my lips.* Psalm 141:3 (NIV)

I believe we all want to live a good and successful life.

Unfortunately, our words don't reflect that. If words have power, that means everything you say is shaping your life. You may not feel it, or see it the minute you speak it, but those words are planting seeds into your destiny. We clearly must be intentional with what we speak, because words have power. If we are going to fulfill God's purpose for our lives, if you want to see yourself fulfilling purpose, you will have to start paying attention to what you say. Words have more power than any of us realize, that's why we often speak them as though they were meaningless. Most believers, at one time or another, have been hung by their tongue. When you take control of your words, you take back your life. Whatever is not your intention must not be your confession. Avoid the trap of negative words. Your tongue is potent enough to either make you or mar you. Do not use your tongue to end your destiny.

> *If you want to enjoy life and see many happy days, keep your tongue from speaking evil and your lips from telling lies.* 1 Peter 3:10 (NLT)

Use words rightly, and you will fulfill God's purpose for your life. Use them wrongly, and they can cause your entire life to go up in smoke. Don't ever underestimate the power of your words; Satan doesn't! He works constantly to get you to turn your words in a negative direction. Refuse to speak anything other than the Word of God about your life and situation, and then watch as everything you've been believing God for begins to come to pass. If your words are in line with the Word of God, satan can't touch you.

One avenue people use to establish themselves in afflictions, pains, sorrow and lack of destiny fulfillment is speaking negative words over their lives. Dr Paul Enenche once said "Until you value your words, you do not value your life".

> *The tongue is a small thing that makes grand speeches. But a tiny spark can set a great forest on fire and among all the parts of the body, the tongue is a flame of fire, it is a whole world of wickedness, corrupting your entire body. It can set your whole life on fire, for it is set on fire by hell itself.* James 3:36 (NLT)

The angels of God are waiting to act on your words and so are demonic forces.

You give the devil access to your life by the negative things you say. Our words dominate us; no wonder the Bible says, *"Your tongue plots destruction like a sharp razor" (Psalm 52:29 SIV)*. We are to speak the Word. Scripture tells us to *"Hold fast our confession" (Heb 4:14 NKJV)*. We have an enemy, Satan, who is against us fulfilling God's purpose for our lives. It is our continual confession of the Word that enforces his defeat.

14. ALWAYS MAINTAIN CLEAR CONSCIENCE

To become a person of purpose you must always maintain a clear conscience. You cannot continue to violate your conscience and become a person of purpose. A weak conscience cannot fulfill God's purpose and plan for their lives.

> *Holding unto faith and a good conscience, which some have rejected and so have suffered a shipwreck with regard to the faith.* 1 Timothy 1:19

A weak conscience is a diseased human heart with dogged arteries. Such a heart won't pump blood as it should. This is likely to cause a heart attack or even lead to death. A strong conscience pulls us towards what is right and channels our actions into doing the right things. So, to consistently violate the conscience is to deny yourself the opportunity of becoming a person of purpose. To enjoy a purposeful life, you must have a clear conscience. A clear conscience is that inner freedom of your spirit that comes from knowing that you are right with God and right with other people. No wonder Paul said in Acts 24:16: "I myself always strive to have a conscience without offense toward God and men."

If we want to discover and fulfill God's plan for our lives, an atmosphere devoid of offense toward God and man is a crucial requirement. A weak conscience certainly will hinder the discovery and fulfillment of God's purpose and plan for our lives.

CHAPTER FIVE

CHANNELS OF DISCOVERING GOD'S PURPOSE FOR YOUR LIFE

The first step in the fulfillment of destiny is discovery. Until you get to the point of discoveries in life, you are likely not going to make a mark in life. In my first book *The Obstacles to Success*, I wrote that "small men are men of small discoveries". "Bishop Oyedepo captured it better when he said, "Everything a person becomes is a function of the discoveries he has made". Ignorance of purpose leads to the greatest tragedy in life. The journey of discoveries is a must in the fulfillment of destiny. To become all that God created you to be, you must consistently go on a personal search. Jeremiah 29:13 says:

> *And ye shall seek me, and find me, when ye shall search for me with all your heart.*

We will look at some channels of discovering God's purpose for your life. This chapter is specifically written to hand you clue to knowing God's purpose for your life. By the end of this Chapter, your life will not remain the same in Jesus' name, Amen.

CHANNEL #1: THROUGH HEARING FROM GOD

Hearing what God wants you to do with your life is key in discovering God's purpose and plan. You can only find your purpose in God, if you want to know the purpose of an item or product, ask and hear from the manufacturer. To know your divine direction and instructions, seek to hear from God. There is a reason why He created you; hear from Him to know that intention and reason. Hearing from God is the major channel for the discovery of God's purpose and plan for your life. Paul heard from God to discover God's purpose and plans for his life.

> *And he trembling and astonished said, Lord, what will you have me to do? And the Lord said unto him, arise and go into the city, and it shall be told you what you must do.* (Acts 9:6)

Hearing from God is a must in the school of purpose and destiny fulfilment. The discovery of God's purpose and plan is simple if you can hear what God is saying to you. God speaking to you directly concerning His purpose and plans for your life is not negotiable. When a man hears from God as regards His plans and purpose, he is sure of the backing of God to bring it to fulfilment. To hear from God is to be a shining light in your generation. What God told you concerning your life and destiny should never be discarded.

Paul discovered his purpose through hearing from God in Acts 26:15.

But rise and stand upon thy feet for I have appeared unto thee for this purpose, to make thee a minister and a witness both of these things which thou hast see, and of those things in the which I will appear unto thee.

God knows the details of your life. The true picture of your purpose can be accessed to Him. So, to discover God's purpose for your life, you must develop yourself in hearing from God. It will be difficult to discover purpose if family and friends are the ones you are hearing from. Don't let your choices in life be solely based on people's desires for you or on popular opinions, but based on hearing from God. Place high premium on what God told you.

To hear from God concerning His purpose for your life, you must ask Him—you must diligently seek Him and hear from Him. You must ask God to show you the things He created you to do. God wants you to discover His purpose for your life more than you do. Your purpose is what God wants to do through you. Thus, to discover purpose, do what He tells you to do.

Hearing from God puts you in divine plan and not anybody's plans. Hearing from God gives direction and location. Nothing transforms your destiny like hearing from God. Men who know the mind of God cannot miss the purpose of God for their generation. Remember you came from God and are passing through this life to do His will. He is ready to tell you what He created you for. John Wesley, the founder of the Methodist Church said, "I am a spirit sent from God, coming from eternity, passing through time and going back to eternity." You can hear from God through His written Word and the inward witness always if you stay with God's Word.

God can speak to you in form of spirit inspired thoughts that are consistent with His Word. Hearing from God requires you to follow the leading of the Spirit, this will point you to God and His Word.

CHANNEL # 2: THROUGH PEACE AND QUIETNESS

There is a future for the man of peace. (Psalm 37:37b – NIV)

Every purpose of God produces peace and quietness within the heart. Peace and quietness are the inner satisfaction released by the Holy Spirit into your heart concerning a matter. Lack of peace and quietness in any matter is likely to be an indicator that God is not involved. It may also signify His disapproval. Whenever you are about to take a step in any area of your life, and you discover that it is full of tension, worry, anxiety and sorrow, check it. That is often a clear sign that the step you are about to take may not be the purpose of God for your life. This is crucial because God's purpose for your life is fueled by the peace of God. The will of God commands the peace of God. Whatever is devoid of peace is devoid of God. God wants you to discover and fulfil His purpose for your life and He guides you to that purpose through peace and quietness. There is a future for a man of peace. Any man walking outside the purpose of God has no future. Every direction and instruction that will lead you to your future, a glorious future, is confirmed with peace. Whatever is devoid of peace has no divine approval and will not lead to a divine destiny.

The peace of God is one of your safest guides into finding God's purpose for your life. Do not do anything that the peace of

God did not guide you into. Philippians 4:7 say:

> *And the peace of God, which passeth all understanding, shall keep your hearts and minds through Christ Jesus.*

When you are in the purpose of God for your life, you will experience peace and quietness in that purpose. When you discover that you are not having peace, not just peace but the peace of God which passes all understanding, you might be in the wrong. The peace of God will take you to your purpose in life. I like how the Psalmist expressed this in Psalm 85:8

> *I will hear what God the Lord will speak for he will speak peace unto His people, and to his saints: but let them not turn again to folly.*

When the peace of God becomes absent, your destiny is in question, and if you pursue that path, it may cost you your destiny. In other words, without purpose, folly is inevitable, and peace of mind is absent. On the other hand, those who are in the purpose of God for their lives are those who are guided by peace that is beyond mortal comprehension. They hardly make silly and destructive mistakes that lead to a life of regrets and misery. Friend, whatever you don't have the peace of God about, query it. Anything that steals away your inner quietness is not worth the

> *And the work of righteousness shall be peace and the effect of righteousness, quietness and assurance forever* (Isaiah 32:17)

The above scripture gives me joy. When you are in line with

God's plan for your life, you run free from any anxiety. You stop running helter-skelter, looking here and there because you are aware of the guidance you received through the peace of God and the assurance that follows it. The peace and quietness are not momentary but consistent. It is not meant to be a temporary relief or happiness that comes when a task is accomplished. It is far more than that. You cannot fake the peace of God that guides into purpose. Your heart must bear witness to this peace and quietness. When you don't have this peace and quietness in your heart, you will always be aware of it. Don't deceive yourself. I like what Earl Hopper said: "THE HARDEST THING TO HIDE is something that is not there." (Emphasis mine).

God leads and guides us into His purpose for our lives through the peace of God in our minds. The peace channel is a major channel for the discovery of purpose. If your peace and quietness is intact in whatsoever you are doing, then you have there an indicator of purpose.

> *For ye shall go out with joy, and be led forth with peace...* (Isaiah 55:12)

If you follow the peace channel, you will not miss God's purpose. Discovering God's purpose for your life will free you from confusions and uncertainty. Every purpose of God produces peace in you. If you don't have peace in the direction your life is going, check it, it may not be God's purpose for you. You will find peace in doing God's purpose. Anything that makes you restless will not take you to your land of rest. Locate your purpose in the areas you have peace and quietness about. Whatever makes you fret may not be your purpose. Remember that you are not seeking purpose for competition. Your destiny will be of little impact if you are always out to compete or live-in anxiety. You are afraid of the unknown because you do not know your purpose.

God wants you to live a life of purpose not confusion or conflict. Thus, the purpose of God for your life will produce the peace of God. God will use peace to guide you into His divine purpose for your life. Colossians 3:15 says:

> *And let the peace of God rule in your hearts, to which also you were called in one body and be thankful.*

The word "rule" in this scripture should be properly considered. The peace of God is a check for us if we must discover and follow God's plans for our lives. Rev Joshua Tende captured it better when he said, "Let the peace of God regulate your decision making." To discover God's purpose and plan for your life, let the peace of God call the shots in your life. Don't act until you are guided by the peace of God. Don't allow your emotions to decide your destiny. Don't allow your senses to decide your destiny.

The peace channel will act as an umpire to decide what needs to be in or out of your life. The easiest way to discover if you are in God's purpose is when you sense God's peace. Becoming a person of purpose is becoming a person led forth in peace and quietness. The peace of God is like a compass for the discovery of God's purpose and plan for your life. In seeking to discover God's purpose and plan, watch for peace and watch out for lack of peace. The latter can be a warning that you are about doing what is not God's purpose or plan for your life or that it is not yet time to do that which you intend to do. Never ignore the peace sign in your heart.

God will keep you in perfect peace if you trust Him with your life and destiny and let Him guide you into the discovery of His purpose and will for your life. Isaiah 26:3 says: "You will keep him in perfect peace, whose mind is stayed on you, because he trusts in you."

CHANNEL #3: THROUGH LOVING WHAT HE CREATED YOU TO DO

One way to discover your God ordained purpose is by finding out what you love to do, that is connected to what he created you to do; that thing that comes easily for you. What you love to do is a pointer to God's purpose for your life. Some people hold the erroneous belief that God always leads you to what you don't like to do. This is not exactly true. Determining what you love to do often helps you figure out what God has called you to do. Let us examine the life of Moses and David in the Bible.

> *And seeing one of them suffer wrong, he defended him and avenged him that was oppressed and smote the Egyptian: for he supposed his brethren would have understood how that God by his hand would deliver them: But they understood not.* (Acts 7:24 – 25)

Moses, long before he became a deliverer of his people, had always loved to deliver people. He loved freedom and hated oppression. He never knew his love for people was hidden in a great leadership potential to lead men out of captivity.

> *Then one of the men said "Behold, I have seen a son of*

Jesse the Bethlehemite who is a skillful musician, a mighty man of valour, one prudent in speech and a handsome man; and the LORD is with him. (1 Samuel 16:18)

The above report shows that David was a man in love with what he was created to do, and that ultimately led him to his destiny. What you love to do with joy and excitement is a clue to your purpose. If you are always happy doing something, it is a clue or signpost to your God-ordained purpose. The things you love and find delight in doing are clues to your purpose. I like the way Steve Jobs puts it: "You've got to find what you love and that is as true for your work as it is for your lovers. Your work is going to fill a large part of your life, and the only way to be truly satisfied is to do what you believe is great work. And the only way to do great work is to love what you do."

Do not ignore those things you love doing and that give you joy and excitement. Watch them; that could be where your purpose lies. When a man discovers what excites him and gives him joy, he ignores the opposition before him and goes ahead to fulfil his God-ordained purpose. Martin Luther King discovered himself and what he loved doing, and he began to champion the course of the liberation of African Americans despite stiff opposition at that time. When you discover what is your delight and key to your purpose, you remain what I call an unstoppable force. The death of Martin Luther only strengthened the resolve of African Americans for freedom in the United States.

Jesus was a man that keyed into His purpose through what He

loved to do. See what John 2:16 – 17 says:

> *And He said to those who sold doves, Take these things away! Do not make my Father's house a house of merchandise! Then His disciples remembered that it was written zeal for your house has eaten me up.*

Stop pursuing the wrong things and go for what you love to do. When you discover what you love to do, you ignore all challenges before you and go ahead to fulfil the destiny God has for you. Follow what you love to do that gives God glory and honor, and then leave this world a better place than you met it. Leave a legacy for others to emulate. There is a connection between deep affection in your heart and the purpose of God for your life. What you love doing is a pointer to what you will live doing. The area of your love can become the area of your purpose. What are the things you really love to do? Don't ignore them; pay attention to them.

To discover God's purpose for your life and destiny, do not ignore what is established in your heart. To ignore your heart is to ignore destiny. It is not wisdom to ignore your affections in the pursuit of purpose. God is particular about what you love doing. What you love doing brings you joy, and God wants you to fulfil His purpose for your life with joy and excitement. When you do what you love doing, it gives you inner satisfaction. To discover purpose, you must find out what you love to do without struggling. When a man discovers what he loves to do and that gives him excitement, he ignores trying to force himself to become somebody else. Dr Paul Enenche puts it this way: "One of the greatest tragedies of the world today is the principle of imitation and competition—everybody trying to be like someone or outdo someone. And so, the world is in short supply of original people. As a result, human needs and demands are largely unmet. Those who are to meet those needs are busy doing something else." This is a sad situation. What you love doing, you will do with PASSION. What you love is what you will be passionate about. You will succeed at the things you are passionate about.

End the stress and struggle today by focusing on those things you love to do. You increase your productivity and capacity by focusing on the things you love to do. Stop trying to do what you don't love to do. You were born original, don't die a photocopy. Therefore, I challenge you to make up your mind today to discover those things you love to do and follow God's plan for your life. Take a stock of what you love to do today and trust God to launch you into your enviable destiny. When you are doing what you love doing, you are self-motivated and self-motivation is crucial to fulfillment of destiny.

CHANNEL #4: THROUGH WHAT YOU ARE WILLING TO DO FOR FREE

What are you willing to do even when nobody will reward you, and you will not receive a pay for? If money wasn't an issue, what would you be willing to do? What are you willing to do for satisfaction and not remuneration? What will you gladly be doing with your life if you had all the money you needed in life? The answer to these questions is a clue to your purpose. When you are willing to do something for free, it is an indication of a strong passion to make a difference. You don't live for money and income but live to make a difference. If for instance counting money at the bank for free excites you, then you are likely doing what will bring you true fulfillment.

When your devotion and commitment is not because of the pay and reward you get for doing something, then it is an indicator to purpose. If you are willing to do something for free, it will never be a burden or stress to you, because you find a sense of joy and fulfillment doing it. The only motivation a lot of people get in doing something is the motivation of the money and reward they get for doing it. But when you find yourself motivated to do something without a reward or money incentive, check it, the purpose of God for your life is calling you. You will find fun doing God's purpose for your life. The reason why you are willing to do something for free is the passion you feel towards that thing or direction. Passion cannot be hidden. When doing what is God's purpose for your life, factors like money and incentives become less critical. You are simply consumed with passion to make a difference in the lives of others. It will be obvious to all around you that you are walking in purpose, because of your undying passion to make a difference.

Becoming a person of purpose is becoming a person for whom money is secondary in decision making. If money is your primary consideration for what you are doing, you are not in purpose. That thing that makes you think of impact and not of income is a clue to your destiny. Money, without doubt, will follow but it is never your priority. Once money and incentives are not your consideration, you are on the path of destiny. Most times, people earn a lot of money in doing something and still feel empty. The simple reason is that such a thing has no connection with their purpose in life. So, to discover your purpose, start paying attention to what excites you when money is not involved.

A true purpose will focus on creating value and improving the lives of others. When you are doing something connected to your purpose, you lose sight of money, incentives and rewards. John 9:4 says, "I must work the works of him that sent me, while it is day: the night cometh when no man can work." Jesus clearly shows us He is working for free and not for any other thing, because He was pursuing God's purpose for His life.

To discover your purpose, it will be important to write down a list of things you enjoy doing. They should be things you love, and which make you happy. They should also be things you enjoy doing without getting paid to do them. Average individuals pursue money, feeding the family, getting old and waiting to die. People of purpose, on the other hand, pursue making a difference in their world. If you genuinely serve your generation with your God ordained purpose, money will serve you. Your money is in you, but you must make purpose your pursuit.

CHANNEL #5: THROUGH WHAT YOU DO WITH EASE

What you do with ease and get results effortlessly, is a clue to your God-ordained purpose. When you do something with ease and people around you are amazed at the results they see, it is an indication of purpose. I like to refer to what you do with ease as *grace*. When you do what you do with ease, you don't struggle to get results. When you do something effortlessly it is a pointer to the fact that there is a connection between that thing you do with ease and God's purpose for your life. When you keep struggling to do something, ask yourself: "Is this God's purpose for my life?" How far a man goes in the pursuit of his dreams and aspirations depends on whether he is doing the things he does with ease or not. Does he have enough grace to function in that area effortlessly? I dare say at this juncture that this ease or grace is not a skill that can be acquired through training, neither is it something you go to school to obtain. Instead, this ease or grace is a gift you receive from God to fulfil your destiny.

Check your life, what is that thing you do with ease and yet obtain great results? Many people are failures in life because they insist on doing something they have not been graced with or something they struggle to do. I've never liked Math, for instance. Whenever I see a math problem, it takes me time to figure out the solution. My wife, on the other hand, is quite good with numbers. She is always amazed at how poor I am with Math. Numbers have never been what I do with ease, and my guess is that they never will be! God created me to do other things with ease. I can write, analyze to proffer solutions, lead and communicate well, and I do all these effortlessly.

You see, the problem with most people is they spend time trying to do things they do not do with ease. You are tailor-made to fulfil your purpose with ease. Paul said in 1 Corinthians 15:10 (NIV).

> *But by the grace of God, I am what I am, and his grace to me was not without effect. No, I worked harder than all of them yet not I, but the grace of God that was with me.*

The easiest thing to do in life is to do that thing you do with ease or have been graced with the ability to do. On the flip side, the toughest thing to do in life is to do that thing you have not been equipped for. When you do something with ease, you will do things in a way only you can do, because you will do them excellently well. Long Fellow puts it succinctly when he said, "Believe me, the talent of success is nothing more than doing what you can do well and doing well whatever you do." What a profound statement. When Benjamin Carson distinguished himself in the operation of the binder Siamese twins in 1987, he succeeded where all his predecessors had failed by separating twins joined at the head. He does his job easily in the theatre, he does his job with ease, no wonder he has gifted hands.

Every shining star in our generation is a product of grace that makes them do things with ease. Grace is the secret of exploits. Men who enjoy grace and ease always have people ask them, "How are you able to do it?" When you do things with ease you don't struggle to get results. Hebrew 1:9 says, "Be not carried away with various and strange doctrines, for it is a good thing that the heart be established with grace not with foods, which have not profited them that have been observing them."

You need to know the areas of your life where you do things with ease and start developing them; it is a route to your destiny. What you do with ease is a product of God's divine ability in your life. It is a divine enablement by God, empowering you to fulfil destiny and become all that God created you to be. What you do with ease is the God factor at work in you that makes the difference in the fulfillment of your destiny. Learn to develop the areas where you do things with ease if you are to become a person of purpose. God who created you for a purpose will sponsor your purpose by releasing grace to do things with ease on your way to fulfilling destiny. So, to discover your purpose is to discover the things you do with ease because the areas of life that you have grace in are the areas of life where you will enjoy ease. Grace is the ability of God that causes a man to do things with ease—the way God will do it. What makes you to bless others is the grace God has released to you for destiny fulfillment.

CHANNEL #6: THROUGH THE PERSISTENT DESIRES OF YOUR HEART

The direction of your persistent desires in life is very important in discovering God's purpose for your life. This is very important because most times these persistent desires of your heart are planted by God, especially those that keep coming to you in the place of prayers and study of God's Word. They are persistent desires in your heart because they never go away. Check those persistent words that come to your heart, most times, they are due to God's purpose and plan for your life. The purpose and plan of God can come as a strong inner desire to do something. These persistent desires in your heart can come as thoughts, suggestions or the desire to do something that benefits humanity and glorify God. These persistent desires of the heart should not be ignored or wasted.

> *And when he was forty years old, it came into his heart to visit his brethren, the children of Israel. (Acts 7:23)*

Moses did not understand why there was a strong desire in his heart to visit his brethren. He was already doing well and living in the presidential palace of Egypt and had all the comfort you can think of. Yet, the persistent desire to visit his brethren will not leave him. He was not aware that the strong desire was pushing him to fulfill his purpose. God respects your desires. Don't disregard the persistent desires in your heart, watch and pay close attention to them carefully. God respects desires. What you desire to do with passion is a clue to your destiny. The desires that will launch you to your purpose are planted by God in you. Wisdom demands that you watch the persistent desires that always occupy your mind. What persistent desires in your heart do you occupy your life with? What path do you desire to pursue in life and destiny?

Whatever a man will turn out to be later in life is because of the desires planted in his heart by God. The direction of your persistent desires is likely the direction of your destiny. What do you have a strong passionate desire to become in life? God has given you those persistent desires to guide you to your purpose. God places those desires in your heart as part of His plan, which means he has one for you. The persistent desires of your heart are connected to the expressions of your life. The persistent desires of your heart are a route to the purpose of God for your life. A person of purpose does not ignore the thoughts, feelings or senses that come to their heart persistently towards a certain course of action.

The persistent desires of your heart demand action in those directions of your life. These persistent desires of the heart can come in the form of mental images or pictures. Do something with the persistent desires in your heart by taking them to God in prayers because persistent desires in your heart are a clue to the work God has for you. Persistent desires reveal divine assignments. Whatever

God assigns you to do, He is sure to put the desires in your heart.

God directs our lives through divine desires. God puts our purpose in our hearts through the desires of our heart. God gives us a glimpse of our future through the desires of our heart. Divine desires are pointers to divine destiny. The persistent desires of your heart are the clue God is giving you for your purpose. To discover God's purpose, nurture the desires of your heart by tarrying in God's presence. If desires don't come out, frustration will set in.

CHANNEL #7: THROUGH YOUR INNATE TALENTS

There are certain divine investments in us that we can engage to live productive lives and impact on our generation. You can call them innate talents or design. By way of simple definition, design entails a man's special abilities, dispositions, provisions or equipment given to him by God. God has a purpose for your life. He also has designed and wired you for that purpose. Your designs are gifts, and talents hidden on the inside of you. They are those things you are gifted to do, and you are doing them naturally. These designs or innate talents at times are hidden inside you. They may be dormant or latent; existing but inactive. When God calls a man to purpose, He gives the man all the requirements to fulfil that purpose. Every assignment has equipment, and your innate talents are those required equipment in their raw state.

What potential, gifts and talents do you have? What is your natural wiring or skill set? These are your design, the provision for your vision. How much of your design are you aware of? Not everyone is gifted to be a preacher, writer, musician nor is everybody gifted to be a medical doctor. What God has deposited inside you is a clue to His purpose for your life, your potential is connected to your purpose. Your innate talents can reveal an aspect of your purpose in life and take you to the ultimate purpose of God for your life. Dr. Paul Enenche captured this better when he said, "What you can do is connected to what you become." Your natural wiring is a major equipment for the fulfillment of destiny. These natural wirings are the provisions for your purpose on earth. When I talk about provision, I don't mean money, I mean the things that are hidden on the inside of you. Life becomes strange to you when you don't understand the things that are hidden inside of you. These innate talents are hidden inside of you, they may be dormant, or you may say they are latent, existing but not active, but you must discover them because the discovery of purpose is the discovery of your innate talents.

Not everyone has the innate talent to be a writer or musician, neither is everybody talented to be a medical doctor. The greatest frustration a man can experience in life is trying to be something they do not have the innate talent for. I have discovered that all a man needs to fulfil his destiny and become all that God has created him to be on earth has been given to him. Whatever talents the man needs for destiny fulfillment has been given to him. The gifts of the Holy Spirit, the gift of men, the gift of resources or the gift of natural talents... just name them they are always given to a man via his talents to fulfil his purpose.

Moses had a purpose to fulfil on earth, but he was not aware of the innate talent he possessed.

> *And the Lord said unto him, what is that in your hand?*
> *And he said, "A Rod.* (Genesis 4:2)

God called Moses to his purpose of delivering the Israelites out of captivity. Moses complained of his inability to carry out the task, and God asked this question: "What is that in your hand?" The point is no one is born empty handed in life. There is always something on the inside, and it is a key to your purpose and destiny on earth. Verse 17 of Genesis 4 says:

> *And you take this rod in your hands, with which you shall do signs.*

Moses carried this rod in his hands for nearly 40 years without realizing that his destiny and that of about 3.5 million people were tied to the rod. The rod in the hands of Moses was that which God used in a powerful way to free the children of Israel. Moses was not aware of the fact that God had given him what he needed to become a person of purpose. Moses was using the rod for the wrong reasons. May you not use the innate talents God has placed in you for the wrong reasons in Jesus' name.

The one-million-dollar question now is: what do you have in your hands? One of the first steps in the fulfillment of purpose is the discovering of your innate talents and endowments. There is something God has placed on your inside. Moses did not know that there was a reserved power, untapped strength, unused success, hidden talents, capped capability, all he could be but had not yet been trapped inside of him. To discover God's purpose for your life, you must learn to look inward. Your God-given purpose is not from you, it is on your inside. God's precious servant, Bishop David Oyedepo once said, "Everything a person becomes is a function of discoveries he has made." To fail to look inward to the innate talents you have is to fail to discover God's purpose for your life.

An American by name Johnson H. Johnson discovered that he had the gift of writing, and he began to unlock that innate talent. He became one of the most popular writers of his time. He founded Ebony magazine, one of the most popular magazines in the world. Johnson was named the Black Enterprise Entrepreneur of the year in 1987.

Anthony Robbins discovered he had an innate talent for writing and speaking, so in his college days, he read more than 600 books in different fields of studies. Today, he is a sought-after speaker around the world. At a time, he was fully booked for conferences and seminars 10 years ahead of time.

You see, the problem with most people is they spend time thinking about what they don't have. I like what Zig Ziglar said, "I believe man was designed for accomplishment, engineered for success and endowed with the seed of greatness." There are no exclusive ranks or classes on earth, there are only men who use what they have by understanding their innate talents. That's how they succeeded where others failed.

Galileo discovered the principles of pendulum at 18. Alexander the Great rose to the throne at 20 and conquered the then known world at 23. Elizabeth Browning became very fluent in Greek and Latin at age 12. You can achieve your life's dream by understanding your innate talents.

Becoming a person of purpose is about unearthing your innate talents. Understanding your talents and gifts is finding God's purpose for your life. The more you become aware of your innate talents, the more you become aware of God's purpose for your life. By discovering the areas of your gifts and talents, you are discovering the area of God's purpose for your life. What are you inclined to do? Your inclination is your innate talent. Don't throw away your talents, gifts and abilities. You must discover those talents, gifts and abilities inside you. Your gifts and talent will make room for you in the journey of life and destiny. Proverb 18:16 says:

A man's gift makes room for him before great men.

Your generation will always demand from you what God has deposited inside of you. Your innate talent can reveal to you an aspect of God's purpose for your life. Your potential is key to discovering the things you can do. Your innate talents are the platform for your purpose and assignment. Pay attention to the things you do naturally and effortlessly. Most times, you achieve a lot in the areas of your innate talents without much training, while others struggle to get results even with formal training. To become a person of purpose you need to discover your potential and develop them through training. Your gifts and talents are pointers to your purpose; however, you can have these gifts and talents and not fulfil God's purpose for your life if you don't engage them.

For your gifts and abilities do help you discover God's purpose for your life, you will need to engage them by using them in different service areas. I like how Rick Warren captured it when he said, "Many books get the discovery process backward. They say, discover your spiritual gift and then you'll know what ministry you're supposed to have. It works the exact opposite way. Just start serving, experimenting with different ministries and then you'll discover your gifts."

CHANNEL #8: THROUGH WHAT YOU ARE DISSATISFIED ABOUT

What does it mean to be dissatisfied? Dissatisfaction is the state or attitude of not being satisfied. It means to be discontented or in displeasure. It is a deliberate refusal to accept the status quo. It is a restlessness in your spirit to leave the world better than you met it. It is a desire to see things that are not working work. It is an urgency to bring solutions to the challenges confronting your generation.

Do you feel dissatisfied or unsettled with your life? Are you tired of just going to work, coming home, watching television, going to bed, then getting up and doing it all over again? Do you feel there is more to your life? What are you dissatisfied with and wondering, why am I dissatisfied? It may be God who is calling your attention to your purpose. God may have placed a holy dissatisfaction within you in hopes of provoking you to start seeking out His purpose for your life. It is my desire to provoke you to unlock the power of those dissatisfaction.

Dissatisfaction is always key in the discovery and fulfillment of purpose. For instance, dissatisfied with the pen, man invented the printing press. Dissatisfied with the chariot, man moves on the locomotive. Dissatisfied with the velocity of steam, man links his thoughts to God's thunderbolts! Dissatisfaction always provokes discovery.

> *Brothers, I don't regard myself as yet having taken hold, but one thing I do, forgetting the things which are behind, and stretching forward to the things which are*

before. (Philippians 3:12)

In the above scripture, Paul was never satisfied because he was always in the pursuit of purpose. When you find yourself dissatisfied with a particular situation with a hunger to proffer solutions, you are on the pathway of purpose. When you find yourself dissatisfied with things that are not working because you know they can work, check that dissatisfaction because hidden in it is your God-ordained purpose. When you are so dissatisfied with the way things are that you no longer accept them, you are ready for your God-ordained purpose. If you are looking for men who will truly affect their generation positively, then you are looking for men who are dissatisfied with the regular life. A man of purpose knows there is something greater than the status quo. Dissatisfaction makes it impossible to be okay with regular life.

Whenever you discover your heart is broken because of something that is not working, don't ignore it. What attracts your dissatisfaction attracts your potential. What angers or irritates you is also a major factor in your dissatisfaction. You cannot change what you are not concerned about. When you get yourself to be uncomfortable about a situation others find comfortable, when you are angered or irritated by the sorry state of a situation, God's divine purpose is calling.

My wife, Dr Ene Egila, as a medical doctor, is angered by a situation where a hospital is not functioning the way it should. When the horrible state of a situation captures your attention, it shows you are the man to solve that problem. These problems will anger you and trigger your dissatisfaction, this dissatisfaction and anger will then push you to solve the problem.

Your God-ordained purpose will always birth a concern in your spirit about a need or problem; you will hear or see something that gets your attention. A burning desire or thought related to the future will generate an emotion. Something will bother you about the way things are headed, and this thought and desire won't leave you. You will find yourself thinking about them always and thinking of how to solve that problem or challenge.

WHAT ARE YOU CONCERNED ABOUT? Anything that concerns you, you can change. However, it will always start with dissatisfaction in your heart. When you are dissatisfied with something, it will be a concern to you. You may lose sleep over it. You won't be able to let go because it won't let you go. Your mind will always be saturated with that matter. It becomes your predominant concern and only a solution will leave you satisfied. J.C Ortiz puts it well when he said, "Having a calling and purpose that eats a hole on the inside of me is what keeps a continual grin on my face."

Don't ignore those persistent things you are dissatisfied with. God has put them in your spirit so that through you, He will bring the solution that will transform your world. God wants to stretch you with that dissatisfaction to birth a new vision that will change your world. Out of the struggles you go through with dissatisfaction comes the explosion of your potential. Dissatisfaction makes you hunger for more and makes you know that where you are is not the best God has for you. Dr Paul Enenche puts it this way: "Progress in life, and with God demands that you look away from where you are to where you would rather be. Let that be your focus."

It was Nehemiah who said concerning the dissatisfaction in his heart, "When I heard these words, I sat down and wept, I mourned for days, fasting and praying before the God of heaven" (Nehemiah 1:4).

When Nehemiah heard about the plight of his homeland in the above scripture, he felt a dissatisfaction with the situation. In fact, he felt it so deeply that he wept. He was burdened by the situation and the burden wouldn't leave Him. He had deep concern for the situation. Little did he know that these deep feelings were the initial birth pains of a vision that people would be reading about thousands of years later.

The point is, Nehemiah's vision didn't begin as a vision, it began as a dissatisfaction, and he unlocked that dissatisfaction to bring about a change and deliverance to his people. Do you have a burden concerning a given situation or circumstance, are you dissatisfied with the way things are or the way things are going? Unlock the power of that dissatisfaction like Martin Luther King Jr did and fulfil your God-ordained destiny. Dr Paul Enenche captures it beautifully when he said, "You cannot go forward by standing still. If you must make waves in life, you must make moves." Don't only feel dissatisfied, unlock the power of that dissatisfaction by making moves that will launch you into your destiny.

When you notice these dissatisfactions in your life, watch them closely as they are keys to that which God wants you to do in life. The problems that make you cry or weigh you down may be problems God created you to solve.

CHANNEL #9: THROUGH WHAT UNLOCKS YOUR COMPASSION

What unlocks your compassion is closely related to what you love doing and which dissatisfies you. The areas of your compassion connect you to the areas of your calling. To be compassionate is to feel deeply for another person or situation. When looking at a situation, what drives you is key. If you are driven by compassion, then you are most likely to solve the problem. When you are concerned about making other people's pain go away, you are likely on the path of God's purpose for your life.

When you find any area of your life where, out of deep compassion in your heart, you are willing to make the sacrifice necessary to make a difference in the lives of others, give proper attention to it. This area of life may not attract compassion from others, but it will certainly attract your compassion. The more you find yourself compassionate about others in a particular area or direction, the more you should pay attention to that area. Your sensitivity to the needs and challenges around you is a clue to your destiny. A heart of compassion is fundamental to becoming a person of purpose. To discover God's purpose for your life, it is important you pay attention to those things that unlock your compassion.

Compassion is a major propeller for the discovery of God's purpose for your life. The sign that something is God's purpose for your life is that it will unlock your compassion. It will open your heart of love to make a difference in the life of others. When you see the challenge, you were created to solve, you feel deep, abiding affection to solve them. Jesus was a man who used the channel of compassion to fulfil God's purpose for His life. He was always moved with compassion to meet the needs of His generation. He was always excited to leave people better than he met them. That compassion pushed Him to the cross to fulfil God's ultimate purpose of redemption for man. Compassion will create a connection between you and the purpose of God for your life.

That compassion in you will not let you ignore the problem you were created to solve. The compassion you feel to bring about change in others comes from God who created you to discover and fulfil purpose. Romans 5:5 says:

> *God has poured out his love into our hearts by the Holy Spirit.*

There is a connection between your compassion and your purpose. The compassion will spring forth as soon as you are in the direction of your destiny. Matthew 14:14 says:

> *And Jesus went forth and saw a great multitude, and was moved with compassion toward them, and he healed their sick.*

Jesus' assignment was to save, heal and deliver all men from the oppression of the devil, but compassion towards the multitude first moved Him. Compassion is the vehicle that moves you to your destiny. Don't ignore the deep affections in your heart. There is a connection between compassion and destiny.

> *But when he saw the multitudes, he was moved with compassion on them, because they fainted and were scattered abroad as sheep having no shepherd.*

Amazingly, Jesus is the good shepherd, God's divine purpose for Him was for Him to be the good shepherd. Yet, before the discovery of the shepherd part of His assignment, He was moved with compassion for his sheep. What is driving you: compassion or ambition? Are you driven by compassion or money and comfort? Compassion will certainly lead you to your destiny.

CHANNEL # 10: THROUGH VISIONS, DREAMS AND REVELATIONS

God can lead us into the discovery of His plans and purpose for our lives through the agency of visions, dreams and revelations. Through this channel you see something that points you to your life assignment or God's plan for your life. This can be by God speaking to us directly or through dreams, visions and trances. We need to understand that dreams, visions and revelations are part of our life's journey. Dreams are one way of receiving fresh mandates from God, however, this must be consistent with God's Word. Visions can be open vision or spiritual visions. Revelation is a result of intimacy with God where the mind of God is unveiled to you.

Dreams can either be a predominant thought in your heart or illustrated stories. They are encoded messages full of symbols that express the mysteries of God to you while you sleep. God can unveil your purpose to you through these images or pictures in the dream of the night. Don't ignore the dreams that consistently come to you in the dream of the night showing what God wants you to do.

Revelation has to do with divine insight into what your purpose is. Revelation puts you in divine plan and not in anybody else's plan.

Revelation gives you direction and location. Nothing transforms your destiny like revelation. Psalm 103:7 expressly states thus: "He made known His ways unto Moses, His acts unto the children of Israel." How much of God's will concerning your life, ministry, career and future do you know? When you know the ways of God, you have access to the revelations of God. When you know the ways of God, you become a producer of the acts of God. To become a person of purpose is to have a revelation of your destiny from God. Men who know the mind of God cannot miss the purpose of God for their generation, and men who know the mind of God will command the attention of their generation. How much you can go in life is determined by how much revelation concerning your future you have. Ephesian 1:17-19 says:

> *That the God of our Lord Jesus Christ, the father of glory, may give to you, the spirit of wisdom and revelation in the knowledge of Him, the eyes of your understanding being enlightened; That you may know what is the hope of His calling, what are the riches of the glory of His inheritance in the saints, and what is the exceeding greatness of His power toward us who believe, according to the working of His mighty power.*

I love those powerful words, and I pray them out every day for me and my family. One revelation from God is enough to launch you into your destiny. If you don't have access to revelation concerning your destiny, you will follow the tide and not follow God. Revelation from God is a major fuel for destiny discovering and fulfilment. Determine to find answers to your destiny by searching deep into the mind of God through His word. Bishop David Oyedepo once said, "I'm not surprised at where we are in ministry today. I would have been surprised if we were not there." This is so because long before now, he had a revelation of what God was calling him to do in his generation. A revelation from God concerning your destiny sets you on the path of fulfillment of purpose. A divine revelation changes the way you think about yourself and gives you your identity in God. It enables you to see life from God's perspective.

Remember, you came from God and are passing through this life to do His will. He is ready to reveal His will to you. John Wesley, the founder of Methodist Church said, "I am a spirit sent from God, coming from eternity, passing through time and going back to eternity." We are living in time and God is always ready to give us a divine revelation concerning our destiny. He is ready and waiting for us to download His will for our lives by getting a personal revelation. Gbile Akanni captures it better when he said, "God has all the time to bear with you. He has inexhaustible patience. Unfortunately, you're the one limited by time. When will you yield to God and start walking in His purpose for your life?

God also unveils His purpose to us through visions, sometimes the discovery of purpose is birthed through heavenly visions that come via divine encounters. To get to know Gods plan for our lives, we must understand that communion with God in prayer and study of the Word is key. Intimacy with God is the birthplace of discovering and following of God's purpose for your life.

CHANNEL # 11: THROUGH MAKING YOURSELF AVAILABLE FOR SERVICE

One of the easiest ways to discover God's purpose for your life is through service. As you serve with your different gifts and abilities, you will unearth God's purpose for your life. Don't be consumed with the desire to lead; be consumed with the desire to serve. Jesus says in Mark 10:43:

Whoever wants to be great must become a servant.

Whoever wants to discover God's purpose and plan for their lives should get busy serving others with their unique gifts and potentials. You may never discover your innate talents necessary for the discovery of God's purpose for your life if you don't engage in service to others. To live a selfless life in service to others is to put yourself on the path to discovering God's purpose and plan. Service to others may not require any talent, but as you get busy serving others, you begin to discover the areas of your giftings and talents, which will launch you to God's purpose for your life.

Service to others shows you are ready to bring glory to God. That desire to give God glory will launch you into God's purpose for your life. A commitment to making yourself available for service shows you are on the lookout for ways to help others and be a blessing to others. This ultimately guarantees the discovery of God's purpose and plan for your life. The opportunities of your destiny are hidden in service. Rick Warren captured it better when he said, "Great opportunities often disguise themselves in small tasks."

When the motive of our service is to bring honour and glory to God, He will unveil our purpose to us. As you seek to discover God's purpose for your life, don't neglect the areas of service you can notice around you, especially in your local church. Deploy the innate talents you notice in you to the service of others. There are always needs around you, so pay attention to them and get yourself in service, especially kingdom services as this will open you up to the purpose and plan of God for your life. The pay for servicing your gift is the discovery of God's purpose and plan for your life. Anytime a man is committed to kingdom service and service to humanity, he gets unusual access to the revelations of God for his life and destiny.

> *Each of you should use whatever gift you have received to serve others, as faithful stewards of God's grace in its various forms. If anyone speaks, they should do so as one who speaks the very words of God. If anyone serves, they should do so with the strength God provides, so that in all things God may be praised through Jesus Christ. To Him be the glory and the power for ever and ever, **Amen.*** 1 Peter 4:10-11 (NIV)

God wants us to serve others as faithful stewards with our gifts to glorify Him. As we do this, He unveils His purpose and plan for us. As you get busy serving others and building God's kingdom, you will know His plans for your life. You will discover the best path He has for you, by serving others and expanding His kingdom. Peter, in the scripture above is asking us to use our gifts to serve others as faithful steward of God's grace. Whether it is spiritual gifts or talents, we should channel them into serving others and expanding God's kingdom to find God's best for our lives. Becoming a person of purpose will demand your services to God's kingdom and the betterment of humanity. There is always a need you can meet with your talents and abilities. Use your God given abilities to bless others, and you will never miss God's calling upon your own life.

As you deploy your talents and abilities to the service of others and God's kingdom, you will discover the unique person God has created you to be. These gifts and talents are not to serve you, but to serve others. As you make it a goal to serve God and others with your gifts and talents wholeheartedly, you will never miss God's purpose and plan for your life. You may have many gifts and talents, but you only have one purpose. As you make yourself available for service with your gifts and talents, you will discover that purpose. If you are not sure of God's purpose for your life, just get busy making yourself available for service to God and humanity using your gifts and talents, then you will discover God's best for you. God gave you talents to benefit others, not yourself. Your talents and abilities are not just for money making but for impact making. You matter to God, and you matter to this generation, and you are the best this generation is waiting for. As you get busy using your talent you will be busy fulfilling God's purpose for your life. In fact, the beginning of understanding your gift is service. Service will usher you to your destiny.

Most of the people in the Bible who discovered and walked in their calling, were busy serving when God called them. God's purpose for your life is waiting for you to engage your gifts and talents in service. Becoming a person of purpose is learning how to sacrifice your time, talents and other resources in service to God and humanity.

CHANNEL #12: THROUGH LISTENING TO WHAT OTHER PEOPLE APPRECIATE, CELEBRATE AND ENCOURAGE ABOUT YOU

Listening to what other people appreciate, celebrate and encourage about you is a clue to God's purpose for your life. You can find your purpose in what people, especially your mentors, teachers, pastors and parents, appreciate and celebrate with you. Listening to your mentors and teachers, especially when they encourage and celebrate something in you is a pointer to your destiny. Your mentors, teachers and pastors are likely not to lie to you, when it comes to what areas they notice you are good at. The opinions of your mentors, teachers and pastors, as it concerns the direction your life is headed, should not be discarded.

Most times your gifts and talents are confirmed by others, especially your mentors, who have watched and observed you over time. Mentors and teachers are useful guides in the discovery of God's purpose. I was encouraged to teach God's word more after one of my mentors, Apostle Osa Aiyemo listened to my recorded teaching and said, "Emmanuel I am proud of you." because I know him to be someone who will not deceive me or lie to me about my strength and weaknesses.

What are you so productive at, that people can confirm you are good at? Encouragements, especially those from mentors and teachers, can give you a guide into God's purpose for your life. Pay attention to the areas or tasks your mentors, teachers and pastor assign to you. Possibly, they are seeing something you are not seeing.

The good thing about your potential and abilities is that they cannot be hidden for too long. So, your mentors, teachers and pastors are likely to have an insight into it. Pay attention, therefore, to what they celebrate and encourage in you. Most likely they are already noticing the direction of God for your life and can confirm it to you. Your mentors and teachers will help you discover God's purpose for your life by guiding, counselling and teaching you. So, it is wisdom to pay attention to what other people appreciate, celebrate and encourage in you.

The right mentors, teachers and pastors can be a great channel for the discovery and fulfillment of purpose. Mentors, teachers and pastors are there to help you grow and become all that God created you to be. Most times your mentors and teachers see more talent and ability within you than you see in yourself, and they help to bring it out of you.

BECOMING
A PERSON OF
PURPOSE

CHAPTER SIX

BECOMING A PERSON OF PURPOSE AND MAKING MAXIMUM IMPACT

God's desire is for you to live an extraordinary life so that you impact the people around you for His glory alone. This is crucial in becoming a person of impact. God is always recruiting men that will change the world for Him; men that will make maximum impact for Jesus. Becoming a person of purpose is becoming a candidate for maximum impact.

Acts 13:36 says: "For David, after he had served his own generation by the will of God. Fell on asleep, and was laid unto his fathers, and saw corruption". No one lives forever. Life is so short, we are here today and gone tomorrow. David made his impact, and we are still talking about him today. No wonder Dr. Paul Enenche once said, "The irony of life is that there are people who have died and cannot be forgotten, but there are people who are alive and cannot be remembered". What is the difference between these two groups of people? It is PURPOSE AND IMPACT. Let your life count for something. Don't waste your life on things that don't matter. Bishop

David Oyedepo once said, "Making maximum impact is about affecting your world positively, it is about making the most of life, standing out among your peers, being unique, a plus not a minus, a contributor not a decoration, a distributor not a beggar".

A person of purpose is a person desperate to make an impact for God in his generation. There must be a desperation in you not to leave this generation the way you met it, but to influence it for good. Until you matter to your generation positively for God and His kingdom, your generation will not matter about you. Are you a blessing to your generation? How needed are you to people around you. What difference are you making? Is the matter of impactful living a burning concern for you? You must make a resolution, as a person of purpose, to saturate your world with all the divine deposit in you. What you carry must be felt by everyone that comes around you. No wonder God's precious servant Dr Paul Enenche once said, "Any life that must make impact, must be lived with the mentality of releasing what God put inside the individual." You can only make maximum impact as a person of purpose if you are ready to put pressure on your potential. Maximum impact is born where you massively engage your generation with your potential.

You must understand that nobody lives forever, and so you have one life to live, and you get to live it once. Therefore, making maximum impact is crucial to a person of purpose. Living to make maximum impact according to the will of God for you is one of the hall marks of a person of purpose. A person of purpose wakes up every day, asking what impact can be made today to bring glory and honour to God. A person of purpose views life as a gift from God to be used to bring honour and glory to God.

Maximum impact is making your presence felt everywhere you go. It is the effect your life produces on the life of others. Maximum impact is touching lives positively for God's glory. Most people desire to live average lives, but people of purpose desire to live outstanding lives, a life of maximum impact. You must want more out of life than to just go along and get along. Making maximum impact is being a force to be reckoned with in your generation for God, a force that even the devil knows that he cannot contend with. A person of purpose seeks not just to be blessed, but to be a blessing.

Maximum impact is the goal of a person of purpose, not just impact. "Maximum" means attainable, the most, the best. "Impact" means influence - the force of impression of one thing on another. Living life at the highest degree attainable is God's plan for our lives. Your life assignment cannot be fulfilled in the grave. So, make an impact now that you are alive. People of purpose don't settle for average. They go for great standing, and they become a standard in their generation. As a person of purpose, your mind should be pursuing something, and that thing is called "maximum impact". Life, like we have established, is for IMPACT and not INTAKE. It is contribution and not consumption.

Apostle Paul was a man who literally donated his life for the cause of humanity as well as eternity. By the time Paul left the stage, he had offered all he was supposed to offer, and nothing was left. Williams Osler once said, "We are here to add what we can to life and not to get what we can from it." Making maximum impact makes life worth living. You must be remembered for something when you leave this earth. That can only happen when you make maximum impact. People of purpose are concerned about how many lives they are changing and transforming for God. They are concerned about how many people are rejoicing because they came. A person of purpose makes his presence felt. Maximum impact involves making a mark that cannot be erased. People of purpose leave an indelible mark everywhere they go. In God's divine agenda, you are the answer to the problem of your generation.

Becoming a person of purpose is becoming a person who is passionate about touching lives positively in every field of human endeavors. A person of purpose is consumed with passion in their heart not to leave their generation the way they met it. Making maximum impact is a burning passion for a person of purpose.

We are about to see a realm of glory in the coming days, that have not been seen before. This generation is about to see the birthing of men that will bring about an unprecedented move of God as have never been witnessed in times past. This will happen at the frequency of maximum impact.

When we are passionate about making impact in our lives, we will see and experience a greater manifestation of the miraculous, greater economic productivity, more effective national leadership, effective, proficient and impactful ministries. God is looking for pacesetters, trailblazers, history makers, world shakers and generational news makers. Becoming a person of purpose means you are a generational solution giver, provider of answers, unforgettable contributor and undeniable impact maker.

A life with maximum impact is not about what you can get, but what you give and offer to your generation. Becoming a person of purpose is about the value you are adding to the life of others around you. Maximum impact is about bringing out the best in the life of others. Making a living is not the only reason for life.

WHY WE MAKE IMPACT

- **We are created for impact**

  You were created to make maximum impact on everyone you meet. You were not created to walk around this earth purposelessly. God created you with the intention of you becoming a person of impact. God created you to live life to the fullest by being a blessing to others. You are here to make maximum impact, and to make a difference in the life of others. God created us to influence the world for Him.

  We are the answer to the decay of our world; we are the answer to the problems and challenges confronting our generation and we add value to our world when we make maximum impact. We provide answers and solutions to our world. We make an impact because we provide answers. Our world lacks light and direction; it is our duty to give our world direction through the agency of maximum impact. Our world will decay if we refuse to make an impact. "You are the light of the world, a city that is set on a hill cannot be hidden." (Matthew 5:1). We are called to be salt seasoning and light bearers in our world through the agency of impact.

- **We make an impact because it is a divine mandate.**

  The first instruction God gave man after creating him was to go make impact by being fruitful.

And God blessed them saying, be fruitful, and multiply, and fill the waters in the seas, and let the fowl multiply in the earth. (Genesis 1:22)

Making maximum impact is an integral part of our lives; it is a divine mandate that God has given to us. We exist to make maximum impact. God is passionate about maximum impact and that is why He is mandating us to go and make impact for Him. You cannot be a person of purpose and not be saturated with a strong passion to make maximum impact for Jesus. There are depths in God you will never discover until you make a commitment to make maximum impact for God and His kingdom. God designed us to make landmark impact; He wants us to showcase His glory to our generation.

❖ **We make impact because we are agent of maximum impact**

God wants to make us a blessing to our world by making us agents of change. The world has needs and we meet the needs of our world through the agency of maximum impact. God is counting on us to make maximum impact.

❖ **To advance God's kingdom and His purpose on earth**

If the kingdom is a priority to you, you must make maximum impact. The success of God's kingdom on earth is a priority for men and women of impact. God is counting on us to advance and expand His kingdom on earth.

❖ **We make an impact because our generation is waiting for us**

We are the solution our generation is waiting for. We have the answers to the questions our generation is seeking. Our generation is waiting for us to turn their darkness into light. The solutions to all the challenges of humanity are with us. We make maximum impact to fulfil God's creative mandate. We provide answers to the challenges confronting our generation. It does not matter about your chosen field of endeavor; you are positioned for maximum impact. If your presence is not felt, then you are not adding value to your generation. It is an abomination not to make maximum impact in your generation because God has provided in you the answers to your generation.

❖ **We make impact to glorify Jesus**

One reason why we seek to make maximum impact is to glorify God always. If your desire to make an impact is to glorify yourself, then you are not making an impact. We make maximum impact to glorify God. God wants to be glorified, and He wants to be glorified through us.

EFFECTS OF MAXIMUM IMPACT (IMPACTFUL LIVING)

I was pondering on the secrets of impact, and it impressed in my spirit that it is in the acronym, IMPACT. Every letter in the word, "impact" carries a vital secret of maximum impact. This I will share with you in this chapter.

I – Intensive knowledge of your maker

Knowledge is the reason why men are of different classes in life. The man that knows this, is ahead of the man that does not know. The rise and fall of people in life depends on the knowledge they have. Hosea 4:6 says "My people are destroyed for lack of knowledge, because you have rejected knowledge, I will also reject you as my priests. Since you have forgotten the law of your God, I will also forget your children." When I talk about the knowledge of your MAKER, I'm saying, how much of God do you know? The more of God you know, the more of God you become. When you know God, you are licensed to operate like God. When you know God and His ways, you become a producer of the acts of God. Intensive knowledge of God and His ways makes you a person of maximum impact. To remain without the knowledge of God and His ways is to remain without impact in life and destiny. You increase in the knowledge of God through search. To know your maker intensively, you must spend time in fellowship, intimacy and communion with Him. To know God, you must know His Word and give His Word utmost priority in your life. The Word of God must dwell in you richly (Colossians 3:16a).

Another intensive knowledge crucial for maximum impact is knowledge of your make. By knowledge of your make, we imply "Who are you?" It is the question of identity. What are you on earth to do? There is a place for you on earth and work for you to do. The crux of this book is centered on the knowledge of who God created you to be and fulfilling it. You have a mission on earth, you were designed and wired to do something. To reach your place in destiny and make maximum impact, you must be filled with the knowledge of who God created you to be. Until you discover who you are, you can never recover your place in destiny.

How do you discover the real you? It is through the Word of God. There cannot be any discovery until you are able to see yourself from the scriptures. You must know yourself through the pages of the Word of God. What is God saying concerning you? That is the real you! Your identity is in the Word of God, go for it, and maximum impact will never elude you. Maximum impact is yours, if you have enough knowledge of your maker, God and what He has created you to do. Your impact in life is determined by your intimacy with your maker, never forget this.

M – Massive action

This is another vital secret for maximum impact. You cannot impact anybody if you are not ready to engage in the instrument of massive actions. Men of purpose engage massive actions and not excuses. "Massive actions" here implies that you go to work, to bring your vision into fruition and not allow anything like excuses to hinder you from fulfilling your dreams. People that will make maximum impact in life, engage massive actions and make no excuses.

Soichiro Honda was a Japanese engineer and industrialist who spent his early childhood helping his father, a blacksmith with his bicycle repair business. Right from childhood, he had been thrilled by the first car that was ever seen in his village. He never forgot the smell of the engine oil the car gave out.

Honda, in his quest to follow his passion, left home for Tokyo in search of a job (massive action) at the age of 14. He obtained apprenticeship at a garage in 1922, where he eventually stayed for six years, working as a car mechanic before returning home to start his own auto repair business in 1928 at the age of 22.

By 1937, Honda had already founded a company, *Totai Soiki*, where he was producing passion rings. His plan was to sell the idea to Toyota. He laboured night and day. Many times, he slept in the workshop (massive action), always believing he could perfect his designs and produce a worthy product.

Finally, after going through the rigor (massive action) to produce the rings, it was rejected by Toyota, because the rings did not meet their specification standards. But Honda's resilience would not allow him to give up. After some years of redesigning the piston rings, he finally won a contract with Toyota.

He worked tirelessly to build a factory to enhance his supplies to Toyota. It was a Herculean task, because Japan was in the middle of World War II, and building materials were relatively short in supply. He eventually surmounted the challenge by inventing a new concrete-making process, that enabled him to build the factory.

The tragedy struck when his factory was bombed twice, and steel became unavailable. Instead of attaching his excuses for the unavailability of steel due to the war, he instead started collecting gasoline cans discarded by U.S fighters. This became the new raw material for the rebuilding of his manufacturing process.

He was undaunted in the face of this human disaster called "World War II" and rebuilt his factory. Then, a natural disaster struck (an earthquake), and his factory was destroyed. Honda sold the remains of his company to Toyota and used the proceeds to find the Honda Technical research institute in October 1946.

After World War II, an extreme gasoline shortage forced people to walk or use bicycles. Honda's keen eyes for technology, led him into building a tiny engine that can be attached to his bicycle.

Due to the shortage of materials after the war, Honda rallied 5,000 bicycles shop owners around Japan to help him revitalize their country. With success in Japan, Honda began exporting his bicycle engines to Europe and America. He founded Honda Motor Company in 1948 and started working towards cheap and versatile cars. In the 1970's Honda developed a small version of engine, and the company started making tiny cars. This gave Honda Company a breakthrough in the automobile world. The Honda brand has become synonymous with usefulness and innovative engineering. Honda oversaw his company's expansion from a car mechanic to a wooden shack manufacturing bicycle motors to a multinational automobile and motorcycle manufacturer. Sochiro Honda was a man of maximum impact, who engaged the instrumentality of massive actions.

The present is the route to the future. What you are doing

today will affect your tomorrow. The diligent do not have the same destiny as the indolent. When you are diligent, you are a candidate for maximum impact. I've had to put in the work necessary for you to be able to read the book in your hands today. Massive action implies you don't sit down wishing to be a man of maximum impact; you work it out. You cannot be related to laziness, idleness and excuses and be related to impactful living at the same time. Impactful living is a product of hard work and not hard sleep. Make up your mind to avoid slothfulness in all your endeavours to become a person of maximum impact. Jesus admonishes us in John 9:4,

> *We must quickly carry out the tasks assigned us by the one who sent us. The night is coming and then no one can work.*

P – Potential maximization

Potential, like we have established earlier in this book, has to do with our gifts, talents, and endowments. Potential is reserved, untapped power, hidden talents, capped capability. There is something in you that may still be latent, existing but not developed. It is a fixed deposit.

You can only make maximum impact in life, if you are ready to put pressure on your potential. Real impact in life is deploying your potential to better the lives of others. Determine always not to waste the giftings of God upon your life. Make that move today, take that step of faith today, to unleash your potential to your world.

To make maximum impact and become a person of

purpose, decide to deploy your potential into aggressive usage. Don't hold back when it comes to the deployment of your potential to your generation. Go ahead and give full expression to your potential, and you will live life to the full. Place a demand on your innate potential. Leave nothing to a life of average performance.

1 Timothy 1:6 (NASB)

For this reason, I remind you to kindle afresh the gift of God which is in you through the laying on of my hands.

Kindle afresh the potentials in you, put them to use and you will make maximum impact in your generation.

A - Anointing

How God anointed Jesus of nazareth *with the Holy Spirit and with power, who went about doing good and healing all that were oppressed of the devil, for God was with Him* Acts 10:38

The anointing is one vital secret of maximum impact. Show me an anointed man and I will show you a man of maximum impact. If you do not want to make positive impact in your generation for God, then forget about being anointed. Impact making is not by empty noise. Empty noise will take you no where. You must be backed up by the power of God. The secret of lasting impact in our generation is the power and the presence of the Holy Ghost in our lives.

The anointing brings freedom, wholeness, restoration and dignity to destiny. So, for you to bring about lasting impact in your generation, you must be anointed with the Holy Ghost and power. To be anointed with the Holy Ghost and power, you must consistently pay attention to God's Word and prayers. You must be massively aggressive about prayers and personal Bible study.

It is known through the scriptures that the anointing of God is a major lifter of life and destiny. The Holy Spirit, the one who gives the anointing, lives in you as a believer. What you need is the recognition and the acknowledgement of the greater one that lives in you. The anointing of the Holy Spirit is to your advantage. In all you do in life, seek to develop intimacy with the Holy Spirit.

C – Character excellence

Character is superior to charisma in human relationships. It has been established that character is a non-negotiable requirement for impactful living. Do not ignore or take character for granted, it is a vital secret in the school of maximum impact. Every great man of impact is a man with a solid character. Character is superior to charisma, but unfortunately today, our world celebrates charisma over character. It does not matter what gifts, talents and abilities you have, once a strong character is not in place, impactful living is a mere wish.

> *But Daniel purposed in his heart that he would not defile himself with the portion of the King's meat, nor with the wine which he drank; therefore, he requested of the prince of the eunuchs that he might not defile himself* (Daniel 1:8)

Daniel was a man of solid character excellence. Character excellence is a choice you must make if you will make maximum impact on your generation. In a world where a man's life is judged by material possessions, it should not be a surprise to us that character has taken a back seat. But for a person who wants to make true impact for Jesus and His kingdom, a solid character is non-negotiable. I like how Randy Macvicar captures it: "Character affects every area of our lives – our decisions, our words, our actions, our attitudes, our goals, and our relationships. In fact, any breakdown in life can almost be traced back to a breakdown in character."

Character excellence is becoming more and more like Jesus in our daily conduct. Character excellence is not possible without a commitment to being a doer of the Word of God. To have character excellence is to be a practitioner of God's Word. You must walk in the light of God's Word to have character excellence. Commitment to living a holy life is the bedrock of character excellence. Godly character is a major gateway for maximum impact, your character is crucial to making maximum impact. Your character determines your impact in life.

T – Time optimization

Like we established earlier, time is one of the most precious gifts ever given to man. As a matter of fact, it is one of the first creations of God. Life itself is measured or calibrated in time, which means time is life. By wasting time, a person is wasting life. It was Vincent Benne that said, "Life is not lost by dying, life is lost minute by minute, day by dragging day in all the thousand small uncaring ways." The Bible also admonishes us in Ephesians 5:16, "...Redeeming the time, because the days are evil." People of impact are highly time conscious. They know time wasters are life wasters. They also know that when you make the most of your time, you are making the most of your life, since time itself is life. The urgency of purpose and destiny makes the man of impact to pray always, "Teach me to number my days that I may apply my heart into wisdom (Psalms 90:12).

Dr Paul Enenche once said, "Those who make the most of time, make the mark in life." Time usage is vital to impactful living. Someone once said "Those who manage time end as stars and those who damage time end up with scars.

An impactful life is driven by a productive life

Everyone was created to make an impact on life. No one is empty-handed in life. No one was born empty-handed. There is something in your life that you can use to make a difference in the lives of others. God called Moses to the task of delivering the Israelites out of captivity. He complained of his inability to carry out the task and become an impact agent. But Moses never knew that he was created to make impact and all he needed to make maximum impact had been given to him by God.

> *And the Lord said unto him, what is that in thine hand? And he said a Rod* (Exodus 4:2.)

Moses carried this rod in his hands for nearly 40 years without realizing that it is God's instrument of change for his generation.

What do you have in your hands? is a question of discovery. To live an impactful life is to live a productive life.

7 reasons why you should increase your productivity for maximum impact

1. **Significance**

   All the brothers of a poor man hate him – how much more do friends avoid him! He may pursue them with pleading, but they are nowhere to be found. (Proverbs 19:7)

Significance means I have value and importance, and my life counts for something. If you must make maximum impact and count for something in your generation, you must give priority to productivity and not just activity. We only have one life to live; don't live this life as a burden to others. Make yourself valuable by adding and creating value. To be considered a person of significance and impact in your generation, you must think of ways of adding value to your world, by becoming more productive. Whatever you want in life, you will get by becoming a person of value and significance.

Once value for creation and productivity is your priority, you are on your way to finding significance in life and destiny, otherwise you will become a burden to your generation. If you have nothing to offer your generation, you will lack significance. People will always remember you for the value you added to their lives. Never think of what you can get from your generation, think always of what you can add to your generation, to make it better.

Each of us, when leaving this earth, will crave to know that we have left behind something of significance for the generation coming after us. But that will never happen, if we are not productive at the things God has created us for. If you want to find any real significance in life, look up to Jesus, trust Him with your life. Keep your heart for God and He will direct you in the paths that lead to a vibrant, exciting, useful and happy life, a life of SIGNIFICANCE.

2. **Freedom**

> *I have the right to do anything; you say – but not everything is beneficial. I have the right to do anything – but I will not be mastered by anything.* (1 Corinthians 6:12)

When your life is unproductive, you become a slave to people and conditions around you. Greater productivity can bring us greater freedom to be who God created us to be. For some people, productivity means activities. If this is what productivity means to you, you lack the freedom it gives. I like how Michael Hyatt captured it when he said, "The new paradigm for productivity is about more freedom; it's about how you can get more done by working less, so you can enjoy life and invest in the people and priorities that matter most..."

You live your life not to please men or make decisions acceptable by society. You are free from the slavery of comparing yourself with others, you are not pressured to make choices or how you spend and use your time. You live your life to the fullest, knowing you are the best God created you to be. The productive person is that person that orders his or her life in such a way as to maximize his or her influence and impact on society.

3. **Satisfaction**

> *His master replied, well done, good and faithful servant! You have been faithful with a few things I will put you in charge of many things, enter the joy of your master.* (Matthew 25:23)

Do you know why most people are not living satisfied lives? They are confused about what exactly they were created to do. They live this life to chance, by trials and errors and remain unproductive at nothing. True productivity and impactful living give you access to share in the joy of our Father God, because you become the Father's delight.

Now, if your life is lacking satisfaction and joy, I want you to check how productive and impactful your life is in connection to God's divine plan for you. Satisfaction occurs when we follow the divine agenda and channel our energy into activities that guarantees the fulfillment of divine agenda.

Well, I've got some wonderful news for you, satisfaction in life is guaranteed when you are doing what you were created to do. Satisfaction occurs when we give our lives to a purpose that will outlive us and make a difference in eternity.

4. **Influence**

> *Work hard and become a leader, be lazy and become a slave.* (Proverbs 12:24)

A slave can never be mentioned as a person of influence and leadership. The determining factor for influence in life and destiny is productive and impactful living; a value adding lifestyle. Your existence on earth must be useful to God and humanity. What difference are you making in your area of influence? I like how Martin Luther King Jr. puts it: "If a man is called to be a street sweeper, he should sweep streets even as Michelangelo painted, or Beethoven composed music or Shakespeare wrote poetry. He should sweep streets so well that all the hosts of heaven will pause to say, 'here lived a great sweeper who did his job well'".

What influence means to a born-again believer, is not the same to an unbeliever. We are not talking about influence for our personal glorification, but the influence that brings honour and glory to God is our delight. If you understand this, then you will make the best use of your given opportunities and talents to glorify God. If you understand the influence you can make for God's kingdom, you will ultimately pursue true productivity.

5. **Promotion and honour**

> *Do you see a man skillful and experienced in his work: He will stand before kings; He will not stand before obscure men.* (Proverbs 22:29)

Productivity, impactful living and promotions are siblings. They cannot be easily separated. Productivity does the work that necessitates honour and promotions in life. Many seek to be honoured and promoted in life but avoid productivity.

The honour many people seek can only be achieved if they are genuinely productive in the things that matter to life and destiny. Lasting honour and promotion in life comes from pursuing God's agenda for our lives and destiny, not from our perfectly devised plans. Seek genuinely to make a difference in the lives of others, and God will show you off! You won't have to promote yourself; others will promote you!

If you are committed to living your life completely for God, pursuing divine agenda, making sacrifices, investing your life on God's agenda and giving God the glory always, you will also always see honour and promotion in your own life. You cannot be genuinely committed to a divine agenda and be a nonentity in life.

6. Personal Fulfillment

> *So, I have seen that there is nothing better than that a man should be happy in his own works and activities, for that is his portion (share) for who will bring him (back) to see what will happen after he is gone?* (Ecclesiastes 3:22)

Personal fulfillment is the fulfillment of one's vision and destiny through personal growth. It's about reaching your full potential, fulfilling God's purpose and building a life of impact and relevance. That's how you can be proud of your life. Every day can be an exciting adventure for the person of purpose.

Some people think or feel that having money and properties, will give them fulfillment. Some think relocating to a better country will give them fulfillment. But repeatedly, we see that nothing gives personal fulfillment in life like following and fulfilling God's purpose for your life. Who you are, defines how you will find fulfillment. It is much easier to find out where to go if you have a road map. Your life's purpose affects every decision and interaction of your life. You can't feel fulfilled, if you are doing something that goes in direct contradiction to them.

7. Giving

> *He who has been stealing must steal no longer, but must work, doing good with his own hands, so that he may have something to share with the one in need.* (Ephesians 4:28)

To have something to share with others, you must be productive. Productivity enables us to give to others out of the abundance God has blessed us with for obeying His principles.

God himself is the embodiment of giving. He gave us life and gave us eternal life through our faith in Jesus Christ. So, He wants us to be like Him by being producers and givers. New discoveries in neuroscience indicate that there is a "warm glow" effect in our brains when we are generous. God has built into our brains a great way to feel happy when we give. We have been hot-wired by God to be givers, because He created in us the ability to reproduce and be profitable.

By giving, we appreciate God for the strength to be able to reproduce. Determine to be a giver by engaging productivity and impactful living. Let humanity benefit from the profit of your productivity through your giving.

PRINCIPLES OF PRODUCTIVITY THAT GUARANTEES MAXIMUM IMPACT

1. **Analyze, prioritize and specialize**

   The light of the body is the eye; if therefore thine eyes be single, thy whole body shall be full of light. (Matthew 6:22)

You must discover what you are best at and have been gifted to do, because that is what will give you profit. Do not do everything; select the best and specialize in it. That is what will enhance your productivity.

Tips on what to do

i. Do that which you feel a sense of duty to do.
ii. Do what will add value the most to the lives of people around you.
iii. Do what you can do easily.
iv. Which one can be done right away?
v. Which one will pay quickest?

2. **Utilize your energy**

   He that tilleth his land shall be satisfied with bread. (Proverbs 12:11)

Work is the backbone of productivity; every product you see is a representation of work. Work is something you cannot see, but work can be measured or converted into products. Energy is what

God has provided for every one of us. The reason why you can hold yourself in a seat is because there is energy in you. There is a law in physics called the law of conservation of energy. It states: "Energy cannot be destroyed or created; it can only be converted from one form to another". Whenever you eat food, there is chemical energy inside food, when you eat, it becomes human energy inside you. So, everybody that has eaten today or yesterday possesses human energy in them.

Now, every energy must always pass from one form to another. Human energy ought to be converted into products. Products are created when energy is converted. Whether you are converting it or not, it will still be converted. Many people convert their energy into nonproductive adventures, such people cannot make maximum impact.

Energy should be converted into products and the way to convert energy is via work. Energy is the capacity to work. If you don't convert your energy into work, you will convert it into something else. You must realize that talking is also energy conversion. While talking, you convert human energy into sound energy. What are you doing with the excess energy you have? Energy ought to be converted into products, so, if you don't have products to show today, it is not because you don't have energy; it is because you are wasting the energy by converting it into something else. Some convert their energy to work; others convert theirs into immoral living. You have an option of choosing what to do with your energy.

> *This command we have given to you, the man that does not work should not eat.* (2 Thessalonians 3:10)

Eating gives energy that should be converted to work. Right now, you are using your energy productively because you are reading this book to become more productive. When you are reading a book like this, that will push you forward, you are converting energy in the right way. Don't waste time. Does your energy convert in studying God's word and prayers? What does your energy convert into everyday? Be aware that there is energy in you today.

> *Drowsiness will clothe a man with rags, the open eyes will be satisfied with meat.*" (Proverbs 23:21)

If you give yourself excessive sleep, you will come to poverty. It is wrong to be eating and not producing anything. Make your life count by productive living.

3. **Optimize your time**

> *Redeeming the time because the days are evil.* (Ephesians 5:16)

Time is your chance to produce every day, the rich and the poor have 24 hours per day. What are you planning to do with your time daily? What are you planning to do with your time this period? A year represents 365 days to produce. You can produce things that will enable you to be a blessing to millions of people out there. Avoid activities that waste your time and life as a person of purpose.

4. **Maximize opportunities**

Whenever ability meets opportunity, the result is prosperity. It is not enough to have zeal to work, it is not enough to know how to manage your time well, you must begin to learn how to identify and maximize opportunities. Ability without opportunity produces frustration.

Most individuals who became outstanding in fulfilling God's agenda for their lives were people of prompt response to opportunities. People began to discover that landlines were limited in coverage and reach, and they needed to communicate anywhere they were, not only at home or in offices. That prompted an opportunity to produce GSM phones. Most of the wealthy men on earth today are men who responded to opportunities they saw around them. Opportunity is not a matter of luck; it is locked in the needs of people. While people are complaining and murmuring about a negative situation, a person of purpose is thinking of the value he or she can add by maximizing opportunity. The critical matter in moving from point A to point B in life is maximizing opportunities by creating and adding value. Stop looking for money and promotion, just be valuable and maximize the opportunities around you, then money and promotion will naturally follow you. When you add value, the system naturally rewards you.

Your opportunity to make an impact is always going to come to you. However, your ability to identify key needs in the life of people that other people are not identifying is crucial for a successful life. True prosperity is a sharp response to opportunity. Like I said earlier, when ability meets with opportunity, prosperity is the consequence. Maximize opportunities by following these simple steps.

(i) When you have a product, look for people to whom you can showcase it. Your ability to showcase your product will solve a problem or concern for someone. There are people who need what you have; look for them. You have the know-how, and they have the need, so look for them.

(ii) Identify occasions and platforms where you can showcase your abilities.

(iii) Become a student of people's needs, consciously watching out for needs in people's lives.

(iv) Be sensitive to changes in your environment.

5. **Conserve and organize resources**

We all have limited resources. I discovered something which is very true: the whole world is moving towards what is called mini actualization. "Mini" means small; "mini actualization" means reducing something. To be productive you must work towards achieving much with small. The essence of conservation of resources is to do more with less in your life, business, career or ministry. This will help you spend less time, money and resources and get more results. A person of purpose does not waste time, money and resources; he masters how to do much with less.

> *When the axe head be blunt, it must need to put strength.* (Ecclesiastes 10:10)

Creativity is what makes you able to do more with less. In creativity, the first principle is having the mind of Christ and developing faith in God and in what He can do through you. Then look for systems that help you achieve better results in the things God has called you to do. Develop personal systems yourself, and always try to get feedback from your progress and continuously analyze it. Someone once said, "I have told myself that if I don't find a way, I will make one." To keep making consistent progress in life you must conserve and organize your resources.

6. Develop your potential

> *An heir as long as he is a child differeth nothing from the servants, though he be the Lord of all.* (Galatians 4:1)

If you have the potential to produce and yet you are not seeing yourself producing, what you need is development of your potential. You will never do what you can do, until you train yourself to do it. So, to develop your potential for productivity and maximum impact, you must become addicted to training. A boy of six years old has the potential to marry and reproduce, but he can't until he develops. Many people have potential, but they can't begin to produce anything until they develop. The difference between what you are doing now and what you can do is training.

Tips on how to maximize your potential

(i) Read books and literature that hone your potential.

(ii) Attend schools, seminars, and training programs relevant to your potentials.

(iii) Get enrolled in a mentorship program.

An unquenchable thirst for growth is key in developing your potential. Never stop growing. Pay attention to development.

7. **Maximize investment**

Money is to be invested and not spent. The more you put into your business, career and ministry, the more productive you become.

PRAYER OF SALVATION

I want to share with you the most important decision that you can ever make in life and become a person of purpose. Nothing about your life will count if you don't accept Jesus Christ as your Lord and Saviour. This is the first step in becoming a person of purpose. If your life must count for God and eternity, you must be born again.

When you become born again, your life will count here and in eternity, but to refuse to receive the Lordship of Jesus is refusing to count here on earth and in eternity. You can yield your life to the Lord Jesus Christ by this simple prayer:

Lord Jesus, I acknowledge that I'm a sinner, I believe that you came to the earth to die for my sins, and you rose from the dead to give me life abundantly. I confess you are the Lord of my life. I ask you to come into my heart and make me a brand-new person. Amen.

If you just prayed this prayer and you meant it, Jesus has come into your life and has made you a brand-new person. He has delivered you from the authority of the devil and has given you dynamic power to live abundantly.

Connect with E E EGILA

(Facebook) @Emmanuel Esuga Egila (Telegram) @eeegila

www.facebook.com/egila

(Website) https://www.emmanuelegila.org